Pamela Thayer

Knit one
S·T·Y·L·E O·N·E

Knit one
S·T·Y·L·E O·N·E

A NEW
KNITTING COLLECTION
FROM LESLEY STANFIELD

Ballantine Books ● New York

This edition first published in 1986 by
Orbis Book Publishing Corporation
Limited.

Library of Congress Catalog Card
Number: 86-92104

ISBN: 0-345-33264-4

Printed in Italy by New Interlitho S.p.A. - Milan

First American Edition: September 1987

10 9 8 7 6 5 4 3 2 1

CONTENTS

INTRODUCTION

This is a round-up of most of my favorite themes in hand knitting. It's a varied collection because fashion doesn't dictate a single look any more and knitting offers such scope to the designer. There are many changes of pace from small, close-fitting sweaters to big, baggy ones, complete outfits and dazzling one-offs. Classics are up-dated to look very new and untraditional.

One trend throughout is an emphasis on shoulders. Shaped and padded or deep and dropped, there's hardly a natural shoulder in the book. The importance of line is one of the features which distinguish today's designs from some of the cosy, amorphous knitting of the past. Another is the availability of interesting yarns. So many new yarns appear each season that the knitter has an almost bewildering choice between sophisticated fashion yarns and familiar basics. Both are featured here, with color another important ingredient. From rich tones through the brights to gentler pastels and neutrals, color strongly influences the mood of a design. Clothes and accessories are also important factors in the style mix and should be experimented with. It's intriguing to find that the same sweater can look just as exciting with a smart suit as with army fatigues.

This isn't a book for the complete beginner, although any reasonably competent knitter could tackle the majority of the designs and the instructions have been made as explicit as possible. Just as important as skill with the needles is the ability to assess what will suit you when it's eventually knitted. Choose your style!

Lesley Stanfield

SMOKY PASTELS

SMOKY PASTELS

ROSE QUARTZ

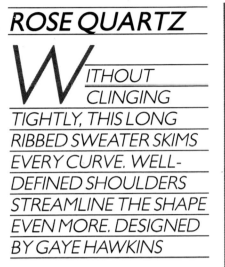

ITHOUT CLINGING TIGHTLY, THIS LONG RIBBED SWEATER SKIMS EVERY CURVE. WELL-DEFINED SHOULDERS STREAMLINE THE SHAPE EVEN MORE. DESIGNED BY GAYE HAWKINS

MATERIALS
10 (11, 11) × 50 g balls Phildar Kid Mohair
Pair each No. 3 and No. 4 knitting needles
No. 3 circular knitting needle, 24 inch long
Cable needle
Shoulder pads

MEASUREMENTS
To fit bust 32-34 (36-38, 40-42) in, 81-86 (91-97, 102-107) cm
Actual measurement – 38 (40, 42½) in, 96 (102, 108) cm
Length – 29½ in, 75 cm
Sleeve length – 16 (16½, 17) in, 41 (42, 43) cm
Figures in parenthesis are for larger sizes

GAUGE
26 sts and 30 rows to 4 in (10 cm) measured over slightly stretched rib on No. 4 needles

ABBREVIATIONS
alt – alternate; beg – beginning; cm – centimeters; cont – continue; c 8 b – sl next 4 sts on to cable needle and hold at back, k 1 tbl, p 2, k 1 tbl, then across sts on cable needle work k 1 tbl, p 2, k 1 tbl; c 8 f – as c 8 b but hold cable needle at front; dec – decrease; foll – following; in – inches; inc – increase; k –

knit; m 1 – make 1 st by picking up the strand between sts and k it through the back of the loop; p – purl; pat – pattern; rem – remain(ing); rep – repeat; sl – slip; st(s) – stitch(es); st-st – stockinette stitch; tbl – through back of loop(s); tog – together
Work instructions in square brackets the number of times given

BACK
With No. 3 needles, cast on 125 (133, 141) sts.
1st rib row (right side) K 1 tbl, *p 1, k 1 tbl; rep from * to end.
2nd rib row P 1, *k 1, p 1; rep from * to end.
Rep these 2 rows for 2 in (5 cm), ending with a 2nd rib row.
Inc row [K 1 tbl, p 1] 15 (17, 19) times, [k 1 tbl, m 1, p 1, m 1] 3 times, k 1 tbl, m 1, [p 1, k 1 tbl] 24 times, p 1, [k 1 tbl, m 1, p 1, m 1] 3 times, k 1 tbl, m 1, [p 1, k 1 tbl] 16 (18, 20) times.
139 (147, 155) sts.
Change to No. 4 needles.
Cont in pat thus:
1st row and every foll alt row (wrong side) Rib 31 (35, 39), [k 2, p 2] 3 times, k 2, [p 1, k 1] 24 times, p 1, [k 2, p 2] 3 times, k 2, rib 31 (35, 39).
2nd row Rib 31 (35, 39), [p 2, k 2 tbl] 3 times, p 2, [k 1 tbl, p 1] 24 times, k 1 tbl, [p 2, k 2 tbl] 3 times, p 2, rib 31 (35, 39).
4th row As 2nd.
6th row Rib 30 (34, 38), c 8 b, c 8 f, [p 1, k 1 tbl] 23 times, p 1, c 8 b, c 8 f, rib 30 (34, 38).
8th row As 2nd.
10th row As 2nd.
These 10 rows form pat.
Rep 1st to 10th rows twice, then work 1st to 9th rows again.
Keeping pat correct, shape sides thus:
Dec row (right side) Rib 4, k 3 tog, pat to last 7 sts, k 3 tog tbl, rib 4.
Pat 19 rows.
Rep last 20 rows once, then work dec row again. 127 (135, 143) sts.
Pat 63 (61, 59) rows straight, ending with a 3rd (1st, 9th) pat row. A total of

143 (141, 139) rows of pat have now been completed.

Armhole Shaping
Keeping pat correct, bind off 4 sts at beg of next 4 rows. Dec 1 st at each end of next row and every foll alt row until 103 (111, 119) sts rem.
Pat 27 rows straight, ending with a 1st (9th, 7th) pat row. A total of 181 (179, 177) rows of pat have now been completed.
Inc 1 st at each end of next row and every foll 4th row until there are 117 (125, 133) sts.
Pat 3 (5, 7) rows, ending with a 9th pat row.

Shoulder Shaping
Bind off 19 (21, 23) sts at beg of next 4 rows. Leave rem 41 sts on a spare needle.

POCKET LININGS
Make 2 With No. 4 needles, cast on 28 sts. Work 4¾ in (12 cm) in st-st, ending with a p row.
Break off yarn and leave sts on a stitch holder.

FRONT
With No. 3 needles, cast on 125 (133, 141) sts.
Rep 1st and 2nd rib rows of back for 2 in (5 cm), ending with a 1st rib row.
Change to No. 4 needles and rib a further 39 rows.
Dec row (right side) Rib 4, k 3 tog, rib to last 7 sts, k 3 tog tbl, rib 4. 121 (129, 137) sts. Rib 11 rows.
Pocket Opening row (right side) Rib 22 (26, 30) sts, sl next 28 sts on to a stitch holder, work across sts of 1st pocket lining, thus – [k 1 tbl, p 1] 3 times, [k 1 tbl, m 1, p 1, m 1] 3 times, k 1 tbl, m 1, [p 1, k 1 tbl] 7 times, p 1, rib next 21 sts of front, sl next 28 sts on to a stitch holder, work across sts of 2nd pocket lining thus – [p 1, k 1 tbl] 7 times, [m 1, p 1, m 1, k 1 tbl] 3 times, m 1, p 1, [k 1 tbl, p 1] 3 times, k 1 tbl, rib

22 (26, 30). 135 (143, 151) sts.
Beg with 3rd pat row of back (noting that there are 2 sts less at each end of (rows), pat 7 rows.
Rep dec row as back.
Pat 19 rows.
Rep dec row. 127 (135, 143) sts.
Pat 47 (45, 43) rows straight, ending with a 7th (5th, 3rd) pat row.

Neck Shaping
1st row (right side) Pat 63 (67, 71) sts, turn.

Cont on these sts only for 1st side and leave rem sts on a spare needle.
**Dec 1 st at neck edge on next row and every foll 4th row until 59 (63, 67) sts rem.
Pat 2 rows, ending with a 3rd (1st, 9th) pat row. Thus front matches back to armholes.

Armhole Shaping
Cont to dec at neck edge on every 4th row from previous dec, AND AT THE SAME TIME, bind off 4 sts at beg of next row and on the foll alt row. Pat 1 row – omit this row on 2nd side of neck.
Dec 1 st at armhole edge on next row and on the foll 3 alt rows.
Cont to dec at neck edge only until 37 (41, 45) sts rem, ending with a 1st (9th, 7th) pat row.
Still dec at neck edge as before, inc 1 st at armhole edge on next row and every foll 4th row until a total of 7 incs have been worked. 38 (42, 46) sts.
Pat 3 (5, 7) rows straight, thus front matches back to shoulder.

Shoulder Shaping
Bind off 19 (21, 23) sts at beg of next row.
Pat 1 row. Bind off rem 19 (21, 23) sts.
Next row With right side facing, sl center st on to a safety pin, rejoin yarn to inner end of rem 63 (67, 71) sts and pat to end.
Complete to match 1st side from ****** but pat 1 extra row before starting armhole shaping and 1 extra row before starting shoulder shaping.

SLEEVES
With No. 3 needles, cast on 53 (57, 61) sts.
Rep 1st and 2nd rib rows of back for 2 in (5 cm), ending with a 2nd rib row. Change to No. 4 needles.
Working inc sts into rib, cont in rib inc 1 st at each end of 3rd row and every foll 4th row until there are 85 (91, 97) sts, then on every foll 3rd row until there are 105 (111, 117) sts.
Rib straight until sleeve measures 16 (16½, 17) in, 41 (42, 43) cm from cast-on edge, ending with a wrong side row.

Cap Shaping
Bind off 4 st at beg of next 4 rows.
Dec 1 st at each end of next row and every foll alt row until 65 (71, 77) sts rem, then on every row until 39 (41, 43) sts rem.
Bind off row K 1, *k 2 tog, lift 1 st on right needle over 2nd st and off needle; rep from * to end. Break off yarn and secure last st.

NECKBAND
Join both shoulder seams.
1st round With right side facing and using No. 3 circular needle, beg at left shoulder, pick up and k 68 (72, 76) sts evenly down left front neck, k st from safety pin and mark this st with a contrast thread, pick up and k 68 (72, 76) sts evenly up right front neck then k across 41 sts of back neck. 178 (186, 194) sts.
Cont in rounds thus:
2nd round [K 1, p 1] to within 2 sts of marked st, k 2 tog, k 1, k 2 tog tbl, p 1, [k 1, p 1] to end of round.
3rd round K 1 tbl, [p 1, k 1 tbl] to within 2 sts of marked st, k 2 tog tbl, k 1, k 2 tog, [k 1 tbl, p 1] to end of round.
Rep 2nd and 3rd rounds until neckband measures 1¼ in (3 cm) from pick up round.
Bind off evenly in rib, dec at center as before.

POCKET TOPS
With right side facing and using No. 3 needles, rib 1¼ in (3 cm) as set across sts of pocket.
Bind off in rib.

FINISHING
Join side and sleeve seams. Set in sleeves. Sew down pocket linings on wrong side and sides of pocket tops on right side. Sew in shoulder pads.

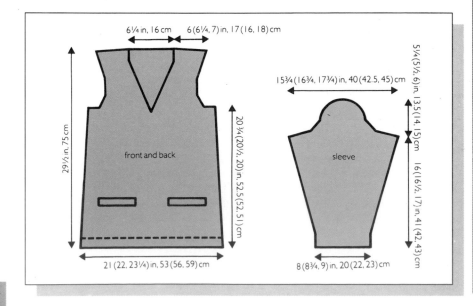

6¼ in, 16 cm   6 (6¼, 7) in, 17 (16, 18) cm

15¾ (16¾, 17¾) in, 40 (42.5, 45) cm

5¼ (5½, 6) in, 13.5 (14, 15) cm

29½ in, 75 cm

front and back

20¾ (20½, 20) in, 52.5 (52.5) cm

16 (16½, 17) in, 41 (42, 43) cm

sleeve

21 (22, 23¼) in, 53 (56, 59) cm

8 (8¾, 9) in, 20 (22, 23) cm

AMETHYST

SHARP, SQUARE SHOULDERS AND AN UNUSUAL TWISTED CABLE ARE FEATURES OF THIS MODERN SKINNY RIB. A CLOSE-FITTING BALACLAVA SLIPPED INSIDE THE TURTLE NECK COMPLETES THE LOOK. DESIGNED BY PAT QUIROGA

MATERIALS

Sweater
8 (9, 10) × 50 g balls Lister Motoravia 4 Ply

Balaclava
2 × 50 g balls Lister Motoravia 4 Ply
Pair No. 2 knitting needles
Set of four No. 2 double-pointed needles
Shoulder pads

MEASUREMENTS

To fit bust 32-34 (36-38, 40-42) in, 81-86 (91-97, 102-107) cm
Actual measurement – 35½ (39, 43½) in, 90 (100, 111) cm
Length – 22½ (23, 24) in, 57 (58, 60) cm
Sleeve length – 17¾ in, 45 cm
Figures in parenthesis are for larger sizes

GAUGE

34 sts and 40 rows to 4 in (10 cm) measured over pat on No. 2 needles

ABBREVIATIONS

alt – alternate; beg – beginning; cm – centimeters; cont – continue; dec – decrease; foll – following; in – inches; inc – increase; k – knit; p – purl; pat – pattern; psso – pass slipped stitch over; rem – remain(ing); rep – repeat; sl – slip; st(s) – stitch(es); tog – together
Work instructions in square brackets the number of times given

BACK

With pair of No. 2 needles, cast on 103 (115, 127) sts.

1st row (right side) P 1, *k 1, p 1; rep from * to end.
2nd row K 1, *p 1, k 1; rep from * to end.
Rep these 2 rows 15 times, then work 1st row again.
Inc row Inc in 1st, *p 1, k into top of loop of st below next st on left needle then k into st on needle; rep from * to last 2 sts, p 1, inc in last st. 155 (173, 191) sts.
Cont in pat thus:
1st row (right side) *P 5, k 1, p 3; rep from * to last 2 sts, p 2.
2nd row K 2, *k 3, p 1, k 5; rep from * to end.
3rd and 4th rows As 1st and 2nd rows.
5th row *P 2, k 1, p 2, k 1, p 3; rep from * to last 2 sts, p 2.
6th row K 2, *k 3, p 1, k 2, p 1, k 2; rep from * to end.
7th to 14th rows Rep 5th and 6th rows 4 times.
15th row *P 2, sl next 7 sts on to a double-pointed needle, turn needle clockwise a half turn then work p 3, k 1, p 2, k 1 across these sts; rep from * to last 2 sts, p 2.
16th row K 2, *p 1, k 2, p 1, k 5; rep from * to end.
17th row *P 5, k 1, p 2, k 1; rep from * to last 2 sts, p 2.
18th row As 16th.
19th to 24th rows Rep 17th and 18th rows 3 times.
These 24 rows form pat.
Rep 24 rows 4 times.

Armhole Shaping

Keeping pat correct, bind off 9 (11, 11) sts at beg of next 2 rows.
Dec 1 st at each end of next 7 (11, 11) rows, then on the foll 2 (5, 5) alt rows. 119 (119, 137) sts **.
Pat 59 (55, 61) rows straight.

Shoulder Shaping

Bind off 10 (9, 12) sts at beg of next 2 rows, 10 (10, 13) sts on the foll 2 rows and 11 (10, 13) sts on the next 2 rows.
Leave rem 57 (61, 61) sts on a spare needle.

FRONT

Work as back to **.
Pat 39 (35, 35) rows straight.

Neck Shaping

1st row Pat 38 (36, 45) sts, turn.
Cont on these sts only for 1st side and leave rem sts on a spare needle.

Dec 1 st at neck edge on the next 7 rows. 31 (29, 38) sts.
Pat 12 (12, 18) rows straight.

Shoulder Shaping

Bind off 10 (9, 12) sts at beg of next row and 10 (10, 13) sts on the foll alt row.
Pat 1 row. Bind off rem 11 (10, 13) sts.
Next row With right side facing, sl center 43 (47, 47) sts on to a stitch holder, rejoin yarn to inner end of rem 38 (36, 45) sts and pat to end.
Complete to match 1st side working 1 row more before working shoulder shaping.

SLEEVES

With pair of No. 2 needles, cast on 49 sts.
Work rib and inc row as for back. 74 sts.
Working inc sts into pat, cont in pat inc 1 st at each end of 7th row and every foll 6th (4th, 4th) row until there are 80 (114, 118) sts, then at each end of every foll 6th row until there are 110 (128, 128) sts.
Pat 35 (19, 23) rows straight, thus ending with a 24th pat row.

Cap Shaping

Bind off 9 (11, 11) sts at beg of next 2 rows. Dec 1 st at each end of next 7 (11, 11) rows. 78 (84, 84) sts. Dec 1 st at each end of every alt row until 74 sts rem.
Pat 49 (45, 51) rows straight, thus ending with a 14th (20th, 2nd) pat row.

1st size only

Next row P 2 tog, * [k 1, p 2 tog] twice, p 1, p 2 tog; rep from * 7 times.
Next row *K 3, p 1, k 1, p 1; rep from * 7 times, k 1.
Next row P 1, *sl 1, k 2 tog, psso, p 3 tog; rep from * 7 times.
Next row *K 1, p 1; rep from * to last st, k 1.
Bind off rem 17 sts.

2nd size only

Next row *P 2 tog, p 1, p 2 tog, k 1, p 2 tog, k 1; rep from * 7 times, p 2 tog.
Next row K 1, *p 1, k 1, p 1, k 3; rep from * 7 times.
Next row *P 3 tog, sl 1, k 2 tog, psso; rep from * 7 times, p 1.
Next row *K 1, p 1; rep from * to last st, k 1.

across these 79 sts. 119 sts. Working forwards and back in rows, cont in pat as back. Work the 24 pat rows twice, then work 1st to 16th rows again. Mark center st with a colored thread.

Shape peak and crown
1st row (right side) Inc at 1st, pat to within 2 sts of marked st, p 2 tog, k marked st, p 2 tog, pat to last st, inc in last st.
2nd row Pat as set.
Rep these 2 rows twice.
Next row As 1st row.
Next row Inc in 1st, pat to within 2 sts of marked st, k 2 tog, p 1, k 2 tog, pat to last st, inc in last st.
Rep these 2 rows twice. Bind off. Press lightly avoiding rib edging. Fold bind-off edge in half and join seam.

Edging
1st round With right side facing, rejoin yarn to the 1st of the 23 sts on stitch holder, rib across these 23 sts, pick up and k 58 sts evenly up 1st side to peak, pick up and k 1 st from peak and mark this st with a colored thread, pick up and k 58 sts evenly down 2nd side then rib across 24 sts on stitch holder. 164 sts.
2nd round Rib to within 1 st of marked st, inc in next st, k 1, inc in next st, beg p 1, rib to end.
3rd round Rib to marked st, k 1, rib to end.
Rib 7 rounds, inc each side of marked st on 1st and every alt round.
Bind off loosely in rib.

Bind off rem 17 sts.
3rd size only
Next row *P 2 tog, p 1, p 2 tog, k 1, p 2 tog, p 1; rep from * 7 times, p 2 tog.
Next row K 3, *p 1, k 5; rep from * 6 times, p 1, k 3.
Next row P 3 tog, *sl 1, p 2 tog, psso, p 3 tog; rep from * 6 times, sl 1, p 2 tog, psso, p 1.
Next row *K 1, p 1; rep from * to last st, k 1.
Bind off rem 17 sts.

COLLAR
Join both shoulder seams.
With right side facing, using set of No. 2 needles and beg at left shoulder seam, pick up and k 15(15, 19) sts evenly down left front neck, k across 43(47, 47) sts at center front, pick up and k 15(15, 19) sts up right front neck then k across 57(61, 61) sts of back neck. 130(138, 146) sts.
Divide sts evenly over 3 needles.
Work 5½ in (14 cm) in rounds of k 1, p 1 rib. Bind off loosely in rib.

MAKING UP
Press lightly, avoiding rib edgings. Join side and sleeve seams. Set in sleeves. Sew in shoulder pads.

BALACLAVA
Cast on 126 sts evenly over No. 2 double-pointed needles.
Work 4¼ in (11 cm) in rounds of k 1, p 1 rib – on last round mark st 102 with a colored thread.
Break off yarn. Sl first 23 sts and last 24 sts of round on to stitch holders.
With wrong side facing, rejoin yarn to marked st and work inc row as back

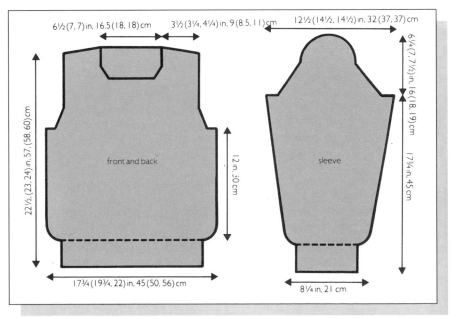

6½(7, 7) in, 16.5(18, 18) cm   3½(3¼, 4¼) in, 9(8.5, 11) cm   12½(14½, 14½) in, 32(37, 37) cm

22½, (23, 24) in, 57, (58, 60) cm

12 in, 30 cm

17¾(19¾, 22) in, 45(50, 56) cm

front and back

sleeve

6¼(7, 7½) in, 16(18, 19) cm

17¾ in, 45 cm

8¼ in, 21 cm

FRENCH DRESSING

BON CHIC

BOLD CHEVRONS DRAMATIZE A LUXURIOUS JACKET, BLENDING SOFTLY TEXTURED YARNS IN MUTED SHADES OF GREY. DESIGNED BY LESLEY STANFIELD

MATERIALS
8 (9) × 50 g balls Anny Blatt Mohair et Soie shade Zinc (M)
3 (4) × 50 g balls Anny Blatt Bright shade Acier (A)
2 (3) × 50 g balls Anny Blatt Bright shade Gris (B)
1 × 50 g ball Anny Blatt Starblitz shade Mars (C)
1 × 50 g ball Anny Blatt Laser shade Blanc (D)
Pair each No. 8 and No. 10 knitting needles
7 buttons
Shoulder pads

MEASUREMENTS
To fit bust 34-36 (38-40) in, 86-91 (97-102) cm
Actual measurement – 44 (46½) in, 112 (118) cm
Length – 26 (26½) in, 66 (67) cm
Sleeve length – 17¼ in, 44 cm
Figures in parenthesis are for larger size

GAUGE
12 sts and 16 rows to 4 in (10 cm) measured over st-st on No. 10 needles

ABBREVIATIONS
alt –alternate; beg – beginning; cm – centimeters; cont – continue; dec – decrease; foll – following; in – inches; inc – increase; k – knit; m-st – moss stitch; p – purl; pat – pattern; rem – remaining; rep – repeat; sl – slip; st(s) – stitch(es); st-st – stockinette stitch; tog – together

NOTE
Starblitz is used double throughout

BACK
With No. 8 needles and M, cast on 69 (73) sts.
1st row (right side) K 1, *p 1, k 1; rep from * to end. (m-st).
Rep 1st row 7 times more.
Change to No. 10 needles.
Beg k, work 14 rows st-st.
Mark last row with a contrast thread.
** Cont in pat thus:
1st row (right side) K 34 (36) M, 1 D, 34 (36) M.
2nd row P 34 (36) M, k 1 D, p 34 (36) M.
Do not carry yarn across the back of work for any further color changes. Use a separate small ball of yarn for each area of color and twist yarns at every color change (see notes on color knitting on page 108).
3rd row K 33 (35) M, 1 D, 1 A, 1 D, 33 (35) M.
4th row P 33 (35) M, k 1 D, p 1 A, k 1 D, p 33 (35) M.
5th row K 32 (34) M, 1 D, 3 A, 1 D, 32 (34) M.
6th row P 32 (34) M, k 1 D, p 3 A, k 1 D, p 32 (34) M.
Cont to pat thus, working 1 st less with M at each end of every right-side row and 2 sts more with A in center, until 30 rows have been worked from **
31st row K 19 (21) M, 1 D, 14 A, 1 C, 14 A, 1 D, 19 (21) M.
32nd row P 19 (21) M, k 1 D, p 14 A, k 1 C, p 14 A, k 1 D, p 19 (21) M.
33rd row K 18 (20) M, 1 D, 14 A, 1 C, 1 B, 1 C, 14 A, 1 D, 18 (20) M.
34th row P 18 (20) M, k 1 D, p 14 A, k 1 C, p 1 B, k 1 C, p 14 A, k 1 D, p 18 (20) M.
35th row K 17 (19) M, 1 D, 14 A, 1 C, 3 B, 1 C, 14 A, 1 D, 17 (19) M.

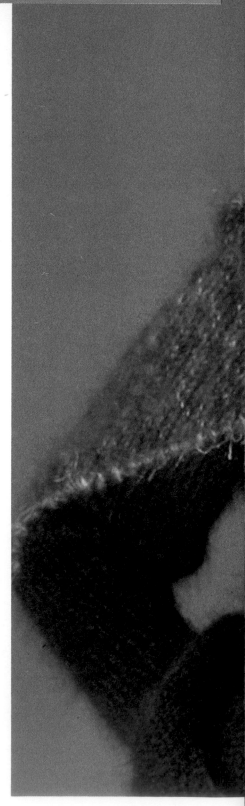

B·O·N C·H·I·C

36th row P 17(19)M, k I D, p 14 A, k I C, p 3 B, k I C, p 14 A, k I D, p 17 (19)M.
Cont to pat thus, working 1 st less with M at each end of every right-side row and 2 sts more with B in center, until 44 rows have been worked from ∗∗

Armhole Shaping
Keeping pat correct, dec 1 st at each end of next and every row until 53 (55) sts rem.
Pat straight until 80 (82) rows have been worked from ∗∗

Neck Shaping
Next row Pat 19 (20) sts, turn.
Keeping pat correct, cont on these sts only for 1st side.
Leave rem sts on a spare needle.
Dec 1 st at neck edge on next 3 rows.

Shoulder Shaping
Bind off 10 sts at beg of next row.
Work 1 row.
Bind off rem 6 (7) sts.
Leave center 15 sts on a stitch holder.

Next row With right side facing, rejoin yarn to inner end of rem 19 (20) sts and pat to end.
Complete to match 1st side.

POCKET LININGS
Make 2 With No. 10 needles and M, cast on 16 sts.
Work in st-st for 16 rows.
Break off yarn and leave sts on stitch holder.

LEFT FRONT
With No. 8 needles and M, cast on 32 (34) sts.
1st row (right side) ∗K 1, p 1; rep from ∗ to end.
2nd row ∗P 1, k 1; rep from ∗ to end. (m-st.).
Rep 1st and 2nd rows 3 times more.
Change to No. 10 needles.
Beg k, work 16 rows st-st.∗∗
Pocket opening row K 10(12), sl next 16 sts on to a stitch holder, k across sts of one pocket lining, k 6.
Work 3 rows straight. Mark last row with a colored thread.

∗∗∗ Cont in pat thus:
1st row K 31 (33) M, I D.
2nd row K I D, p 31 (33) M.
3rd row K 30 (32) M, I D, I A.
4th row P I A, k I D, p 30 (32) M.
Cont in pat, working 1 st less with M and 1 st more with A on every right-side row until 30 rows have been worked from ∗∗∗.
31st row K 16 (18) M, I D, I 4 A, I C.
32nd row K I C, p 14 A, k I D, p 16 (18) M.
33rd row K 15 (17) M, I D, I 4 A, I C, IB.
34th row P I B, k I C, p 14 A, k I D, p 15 (17) M.
35th row K 14 (16) M, I D, I 4 A, I C, 2 B.
36th row P 2 B, k I C, p 14 A, k I D, p 14 (16) M.
37th row K 13 (15) M, I D, I 4 A, I C, 3 B.
38th row P 3 B, k I C, p 14 A, k I D, p 13 (15) M.

Armhole Shaping
Cont pat, dec 1 st at beg of next row, then dec 1 st at this edge on every row until 24 (25) sts rem.
Pat straight until 62 (64) rows have been worked from ∗∗∗.

Neck Shaping
Next row Pat 20 (21) sts, turn.
Keeping pat correct, cont on these sts only.
Leave rem sts on a stitch holder.
Dec 1 st at beg of next row, then dec 1 st at this edge on alt rows until 16 (17) sts rem.
Pat straight until front matches back to shoulder, ending at side edge.

Shoulder Shaping
Bind off 10 sts at beg of next row.
Work 1 row.
Bind off rem 6 (7) sts.

RIGHT FRONT
Work as left front to ∗∗.
Pocket Opening row K 6, sl next 16 sts on to a stitch holder, k across sts of one pocket lining, k 10 (12).
Work 3 rows straight. Mark last row with a colored thread.
∗∗∗ Cont in pat thus:
1st row K I D, 31 (33) M.
2nd row P 31 (33) M, k I D.
3rd row K I A, I D, 30 (32) M.
4th row P 30 (32) M, k I D, p I A.
Cont in pat until 30 rows have been

worked from ***.
31st row K 1 C, 14 A, 1 D, 16 (18) M.
32nd row P 16 (18) M, k 1 D, p 14 A, k 1 C.
33rd row K 1 B, 1 C, 14 A, 1 D, 15 (17) M.
34th row P 15 (17) M, k 1 D, p 14 A, k 1 C, p 1 B.
Cont in pat until 38 rows have been worked from ***.

Armhole Shaping

Cont in pat, dec 1 st at end of next row, then dec 1 st at this edge on every row until 24 (25) sts rem.
Pat straight until 62 (64) rows have been worked from ***.

Neck Shaping

Next row Pat 4 sts and sl these 4 sts on to a stitch holder, pat 20 (21) sts.
Dec 1 st at end of next row, then dec 1 st at this edge on alt rows until 16 (17) sts rem.
Complete to match left front.

SLEEVES

With No. 8 needles and M, cast on 20 (33) sts.
Work 8 rows as beg of back.
Change to No. 10 needles.
Beg with a k row, work 12 rows st-st (lengthening or shortening sleeves here if necessary).
Mark last row with a contrast thread.
* Inc 1 st at each end of next and every 4th row until 14 rows have been worked from *.
Cont in pat thus:
1st row K 18 (20) M, 1 D, 18 (20) M.
2nd row P 18 (20) M, k 1 D, p 18 (20) M.
3rd row Inc 1 st at each end of row, k 18 (20) M, 1 D, 1 A, 1 D, 18 (20) M.
4th row P 18 (20) M, k 1 D, p 1 A, k 1 D, p 18 (20) M.
Cont in pat, working 1 st less with M at each end of every right-side row and 2 st more with A in center. AT THE SAME TIME inc 1 st at each end of every 4th row until there are 49 (53) sts.
Pat 3 rows straight.
Inc 1 st at each end of next and every alt row until there are 61 (65) sts, ending with a wrong-side row.

Cap Shaping

Dec 1 st at each end of every row until 45 (49) sts rem.
Bind off loosely.

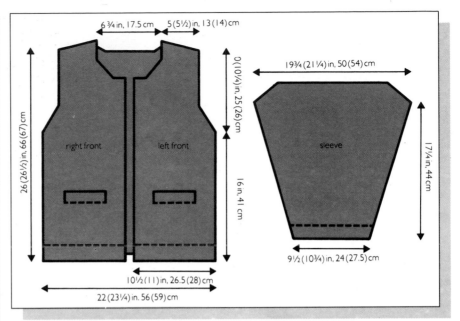

POCKET TOPS

With right side facing, using No. 8 needles and M, work 8 rows m-st as left front across sts on stitch holder.
Bind off in m-st.

LEFT FRONT BAND

With No. 8 needles and M, cast on 6 sts.
Work in m-st as left front until band fits front to neck shaping, ending with a right-side row.
Break yarn and leave sts on holder.
Starting ¾ in (2 cm) from lower edge, mark position of 6 buttons along band and allowing for 7th to occur on 4th and 5th rows of neckband.

RIGHT FRONT BAND

As left, working 6 buttonholes to correspond with markers but ending with a wrong-side row.
Work buttonhole thus:
1st row M-st 2, bind off 2, m-st 2, including st already on needle.
2nd row M-st 2, bind on 2, m-st 2.
Leave sts on a stitch holder.
Do not break yarn.

NECKBAND

Join shoulder seams.
With No. 8 needles and M, with right side of work facing, m-st 5 sts of right front band, p tog last st of band and 1st st of right neck, k 3 rem sts from holder, pick up and k 18 (20) sts round side neck, k 15 sts from back neck, pick up and k 18 (20) sts round side neck, k 3 sts from neck holder, p tog last st of left neck and 1st st of left

front band, m-st rem sts of band. 69 (73) sts.
2nd and 3rd rows M-st as set.
4th row M-st 12, k 3 tog, m-st 7 (9), k 3 tog, m-st 19, k 3 tog, m-st 7 (9), k 3 tog, m-st 8, bind off 2, m-st to end.
5th row M-st 2, cast on 2, m-st to end.
Work 2 rows m-st.
Bind off in m-st.

FINISHING

Press lightly. Sew on front bands. Sew down pocket linings on wrong side and sides of pocket tops on right side. Set in sleeves. Sew side and sleeve seams. Sew on buttons. Sew in shoulder pads. The long 'snarls' of Laser can be teased out with a needle for an extra textured effect.

COUNTRY CALENDAR

COUNTRY CALENDAR

SYCAMORE

CLOUD OF SOFT MOHAIR IS ETCHED WITH AUTUMN LEAVES AND EDGED WITH TWISTED RIB. DESIGNED BY LESLEY STANFIELD

MATERIALS
9 × 50 g balls Jaeger Mohair Gold
Pair each No. 5 and No. 7 knitting needles

MEASUREMENTS
One size, to fit up to bust 40 in, 102 cm
Actual measurement – 45 in, 114 cm
Length – 24¾ in, 63 cm approx
Sleeve length – 17 in, 43 cm

GAUGE
16 sts and 22 rows to 4 in (10 cm) over rev st-st on No. 7 needles

ABBREVIATIONS
alt – alternate; beg – beginning; cm – centimeters; cont – continue; dec – decrease; foll – following; in – inches; inc – increase; k – knit; p – purl; pat – pattern; psso – pass slipped stitch over; rem – remain(ing); rep – repeat; rev st-st – reverse stockinette stitch; sl – slip; st(s) – stitch(es); t 2 – k into front of 2nd st on left-hand needle then k into front of 1st st slipping both sts off left-hand needle tog; tbl – through back of loop; tog – together; yo – yarn over needle

NOTE
When working from charts read rows alternately from right to left (all right-side rows) then left to right (all wrong-side rows).

Take care not to work too tightly into sts that are worked tbl (through back of loop), as they should separate and 'ladder' when work is pressed

BACK
With No. 5 needles, cast on 91 sts.
1st rib row (right side) P 1, * t 2, p 1; rep from * to end.
2nd rib row K 1, *p 2, k 1; rep from * to end.
Rep 1st and 2nd rib rows until work measures 3 in (8 cm), ending with a 2nd rib row and inc 1 st at each end of last row. 93 sts.
Change to No. 7 needles.
Beg p, work 10 rows in rev st-st.

Small leaf pat
1st row (right side) P 12, *work 13 sts of row 1 of Chart 1, p 1; rep from * twice, work 13 sts of row 1 of Chart 1, p 26.
2nd row K 26, *work 13 sts of row 2 of Chart 1, k 1; rep from * twice, work 13 sts of row 2 of Chart 1, k 12.
3rd to 22nd rows As 1st and 2nd rows but working rows 3 to 22 of chart.

Long leaf pat
1st row (right side) P 19, *work 13 sts of row 1 of Chart 2, p 1; rep from * 3 times, work 13 sts of row 1 of Chart 2, p 5.
2nd row K 5, *work 13 sts of row 2 of Chart 2, k 1; rep from * 3 times, work 13 sts of row 2 of Chart 2, k 19.
3rd to 31st rows As 1st and 2nd rows but working rows 3 to 31 of chart.
Beg k, work 3 rows in rev st-st.

Large leaf pat
1st row (right side) P 5, work 27 sts of row 1 of Chart 3, p 1, work 27 sts of row 1 of Chart 3, p 33.
2nd row K 33, work 27 sts of row 2 of Chart 3, k 1, work 27 sts of row 2 of Chart 3, k 5.
3rd to 35th rows As 1st and 2nd rows but working rows 3 to 35 of chart **.
Beg k, work 19 rows in rev st-st.

Shoulder Shaping
P 83, turn, sl 1, k 72, turn, sl 1, p 62, turn, sl 1, k 52, turn, sl 1, p 41, turn, sl 1, k 30.
Sl all 93 sts on to a spare needle.

FRONT
Work as back to **.
Beg k, work 5 rows in rev st-st.

Neck Shaping
Next row P 37, turn. Cont on these sts only for 1st side and leave rem sts on a spare needle.
Dec 1 st at neck edge on the next 6 rows. 31 sts.
Work 4 rows straight, thus ending with a p row.

Shoulder Shaping
K 21, turn, sl 1, p to end, k 11, turn, sl 1, p to end.

Eyelet band
1st row (wrong side) P across all 31 sts of shoulder.
2nd row K 1, * yo sl 1, k 1, psso; rep from * to end.
3rd row P.
Leave 31 sts on a spare needle.
With right side facing, sl center 19 sts on to a stitch holder, rejoin yarn to inner end of rem 37 sts and complete to match 1st side.

SLEEVES
With No. 5 needles, cast on 43 sts.
Rib 3 in (8 cm) as at beg of back, but end with a 1st rib row and omit increases.
Inc row K twice into 1st, *p 2, k 1, p 2, k twice into next st; rep from * to end. 51 sts.
Change to No. 7 needles.
Beg p, work 6 rows in rev st-st, inc 1 at each end of 1st and 5th rows. 55 sts.

Long leaf pat
1st row (right side) P 14, *work 13 sts of row 1 of Chart 2, p 1; rep from * once, work 13 sts of row 1 of Chart 2.
2nd row *Work 13 sts of row 2 of

S·Y·C·A·M·O·R·E

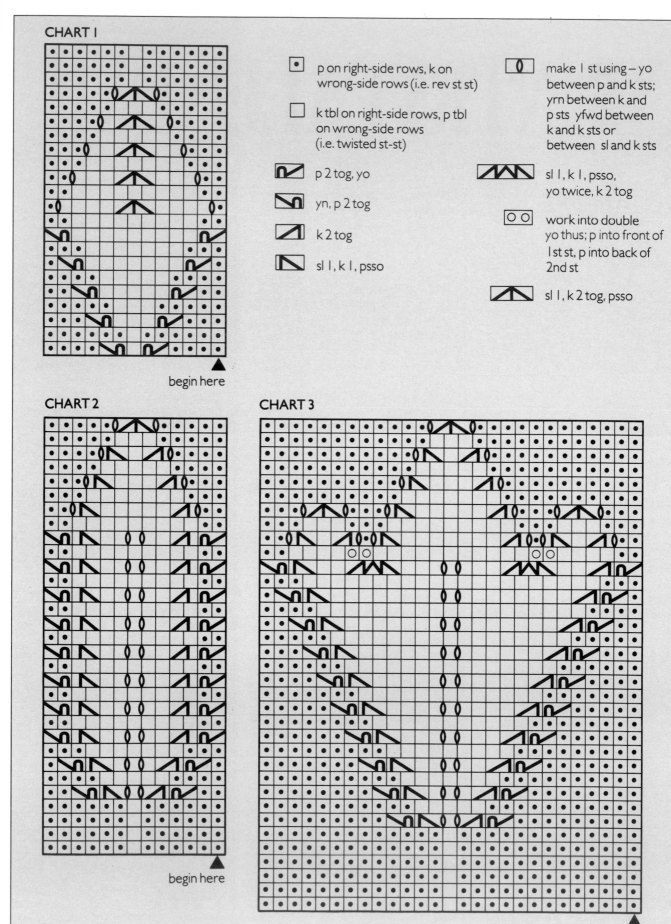

CHART 1

begin here

⊡	p on right-side rows, k on wrong-side rows (i.e. rev st st)	
☐	k tbl on right-side rows, p tbl on wrong-side rows (i.e. twisted st-st)	
	p 2 tog, yo	
	yn, p 2 tog	
	k 2 tog	
	sl 1, k 1, psso	

make 1 st using – yo between p and k sts; yrn between k and p sts yfwd between k and k sts or between sl and k sts

sl 1, k 1, psso, yo twice, k 2 tog

work into double yo thus; p into front of 1st st, p into back of 2nd st

sl 1, k 2 tog, psso

CHART 2

begin here

CHART 3

begin here

right sides tog, and needles parallel, with No. 7 needle k 1 st from each needle tog, AND AT THE SAME TIME, bind off 31 sts.

With right side facing and using No. 5 needles, pick up and k 16 sts down left front neck (including eyelet band), k 19 sts at center front, pick up and k 16 sts up right front neck then k across first 31 sts of back neck. 82 sts.

Beg with 2nd rib row, rib 2 in (5 cm) as at beg of back.

Bind off very loosely in rib.

FINISHING

Join left shoulder as right by binding off sts tog. Press carefully, opening out all leaf sts to form 'veins'. Join ends of neckband, then fold neckband in half on to wrong side and sew down. With center bind-off edge of sleeves to shoulder seams, sew on sleeves. Join side and sleeve seams. Press seams.

Chart 2, k 1; rep from * once, work 13 sts of row 2 of Chart 2, k 14.

3rd to 31st rows Inc 1 st at each end of next row and every foll 4th row, work as 1st and 2nd rows but working rows 3 to 31 of chart. (N.B. Work inc sts in rev st-st).

It may help to mark 1st of 1st pat rep and last st of last rep with a contrast thread and carry this up the work every row so that the extra sts at each side can be counted easily.
Beg k, and inc as before, work 5 rows in rev st-st. 73 sts.

Small leaf pat

1st row (right side) P 2, *work 13 sts of row 1 of Chart 1, p 1; rep from * twice, work 13 sts of row 1 of Chart 1, p 16.

2nd row K 16, *work 13 sts of row 2 of Chart 1, k 1; rep from * twice, work 13 sts of row 2 of Chart 1, k 2.

3rd to 22nd rows Inc as before, work as 1st and 2nd rows, but working rows 3 to 22 of chart.

Cont in rev st-st, inc as before, until there are 89 sts.

Cont straight until sleeve measures 16½ in (42 cm) from cast-on edge, ending with a p row.

Eyelet band

Work 1st to 3rd rows as given for front shoulder, working over all 89 sts of sleeve.

Bind off loosely purl-wise.

NECKBAND

Join right shoulder seam thus: with

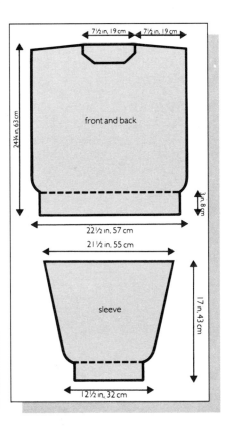

7½ in, 19 cm 7½ in, 19 cm

front and back

24¾ in, 63 cm

3 in, 8 cm

22½ in, 57 cm

21½ in, 55 cm

sleeve

17 in, 43 cm

12½ in, 32 cm

SILVER BIRCH

CABLED IN HEAVY SILK, A TRACERY OF WINTER BRANCHES GLEAMS AND DRAPES SUPERBLY. DESIGNED BY MELODY GRIFFITHS

MATERIALS

750 g (800 g, 900 g, 950 g) Maxwell Cartlidge Aran Silk
Pair each No. 5 and No. 7 knitting needles
Cable needle

MEASUREMENTS

To fit bust 32 (34, 36, 38) in, 81 (86, 91, 97) cm
Actual measurement – 42 (43½, 45½, 47) in, 107 (111, 116, 120) cm
Length – 21¼ (21¼, 22½, 22½) in 54 (54, 57, 57) cm
Sleeve length – 18 in, 46 cm
Figures in parenthesis are for larger sizes

GAUGE

18 sts and 22 rows to 4 in (10 cm) over st-st on No. 7 needles

NOTE

In wear gauge of garment may differ, thus measurements may vary slightly from those above

ABBREVIATIONS

beg – beginning; cm – centimeters; cont – continue; dec – decrease; in – inches; k – knit; m 1 – make 1 st by picking up the strand between sts and on right-side rows p it through the back of the loop or on wrong-side rows k it through the back of the loop; p – purl; pat – pattern; rem – remaining; rep – repeat; rev st-st – reverse stockinette stitch; sl – slip; st(s) – stitch(es); st-st – stockinette stitch; tog – together

BACK

With No. 5 needles, cast on 98 (102, 106, 110) sts.
1st rib row (right side) K 2, *p 2, k 2; rep from * to end.
2nd rib row P 2, *k 2, p 2; rep from * to end.

Rep 1st and 2nd rib rows 9 times.
Change to No. 7 needles.
**Next row K 6, p 86 (90, 94, 98), k 6.
Next row P 6, k 86 (90, 94, 98), p 6 ******.
Rep last 2 rows 2 (2, 4, 4) times.
Cont in pat thus:
1st row (right side) K 6, p 8 (10, 12, 14); reading row 1 of Chart 1 from right to left work over next 70 sts thus – p 11, k 4, p 10, k 6, p 8, k 6, p 10, k 4, p 11; p 8 (10, 12, 14), k 6.
2nd row P 6, k 8 (10, 12, 14); reading row 2 of Chart 1 from left to right work over next 70 sts thus – k 11, p 4, k 10, p 6, k 8, p 6, k 10, p 4, k 11; k 8 (10, 12, 14), p 6.

Cont in this way until all 80 rows of chart have been worked.
Work from ****** to ****** 1 (1, 2, 2) times.
Cont in st-st *******.
Beg with a k row, work 10 rows.

Neck Shaping

1st row K 37 (38, 39, 40), turn.
Cont on these sts only for 1st side.
Dec 1 st at neck edge on the next 4 rows. 33 (34, 35, 36) sts.
Work 2 rows straight. Leave sts on a spare needle.
Next row With right side facing, sl center 24 (26, 28, 30) sts on to a stitch

SILVER BIRCH

COUNTRY CALENDAR

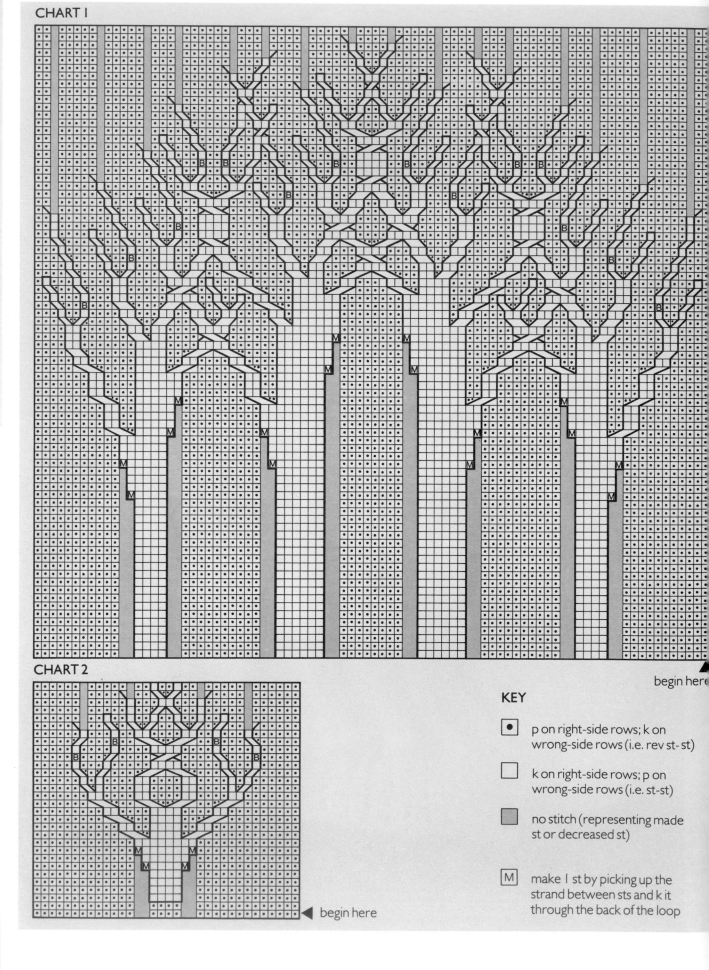

CHART 1

CHART 2

begin here

begin here

KEY

- ⊡ p on right-side rows; k on wrong-side rows (i.e. rev st-st)

- ☐ k on right-side rows; p on wrong-side rows (i.e. st-st)

- ▨ no stitch (representing made st or decreased st)

- Ⓜ make 1 st by picking up the strand between sts and k it through the back of the loop

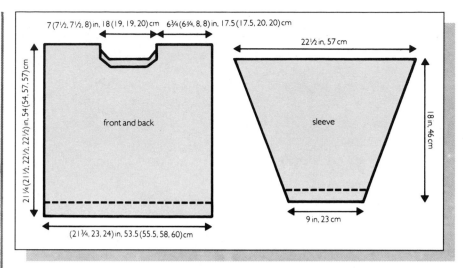

Symbol	Description
	k into back of st
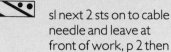	sl next 2 sts on to cable needle and leave at back of work, k 2 then p 2 from cable needle
	sl next 2 sts on to cable needle and leave at front of work, p 2 then k 2 from cable needle
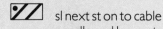	sl next st on to cable needle and leave at back of work, k 1 then p st from cable needle
	sl next st on to cable needle and leave at front of work, p 1 then k st from cable needle
	sl next 2 sts on to cable needle and leave at back of work, k 2 then k 2 from cable needle
	sl next 2 sts on to cable needle and leave at front of work, k 2 then k 2 from cable needle
	sl next st on to cable needle and leave at back of work, k 2 then p st from cable needle
	sl next 2 sts on to cable needle and leave at front of work, p 1 then k 2 from cable needle
	sl next st on to cable needle and leave at back of work, k 1 then k st from cable needle
	sl next st on to cable needle and leave at front of work, k 1 then k st from cable needle
	p 2 tog
	sl 1, p 1, pass slipped stitch over

holder, rejoin yarn to inner end of rem 37 (38, 39, 40) sts and k to end. Complete to match 1st side.

FRONT
Work as back to ***.
Beg with a k row, work 4 rows.

Neck Shaping
Work as for back but after completing shaping work 8 rows straight instead of 2.

SLEEVES
With No. 5 needles, cast on 42 sts.
Rib 10 rows as at beg of back.
Change to No. 7 needles.
Cont in pat thus:
1st row (right side) K 6, reading row 1 of Chart 2 from right to left work 30 sts, k 6.
2nd row P 6, reading row 2 of Chart 2 from left to right work 30 sts, p 6.
3rd row K 6, m 1, reading row 3 of Chart 2 from right to left work 30 sts, m 1, k 6.
Cont in this way, working m 1 inside st-st borders at each end of every 3rd row until there are 102 sts, working extra sts in rev st-st – thus 3rd rep of chart has been completed.
Next row K 6, p 90, k 6.
Next row P 6, k 90, p 6.
Bind off loosely.

NECKBAND
Join right shoulder seam using No. 7 needle thus: place wrong sides tog and with front facing, bind off both sets of sts tog knit-wise taking 1 st from each needle tog each time.
With right side facing and No. 5 needles, pick up and k 12 sts evenly down left front neck, k across 24 (26, 28, 30) sts at center front, pick up and k 12 sts up right front neck and 7 sts down right back neck, k across 24 (26, 28, 30) sts at center back then pick up and k 7 sts up left back neck. 86 (90, 94, 98) sts.
Beg with 2nd rib row, rib 9 rows as at beg of back.
Bind off loosely knit-wise.

FINISHING
Join left shoulder as for right shoulder. When joining seams always take 1 st from each side into seam to match ribs. Join neckband seam. Place markers on side edges of back and front 11 in (28 cm) from shoulder seams. With center of bind-off edge of sleeves to shoulder seams, sew on sleeves between markers. Press lightly with a barely damp cloth omitting rib. Join side and sleeve seams.

STAR GAZER

STAR GAZER

NORTHERN LIGHTS

*S*NUGGLE INTO A GIGANTIC, WARM SWEATER, SPLASHED WITH SCANDINAVIAN STARS AND TOP IT WITH A TASSELLED CAP. DESIGNED BY MELODY GRIFFITHS

MATERIALS
Samband Lopi
5 × 100 g balls yellow, shade 067 (M)
5 × 100 g balls royal, shade 069 (A)
3 × 100 g balls navy, shade 075 (B)
1 × 100 g ball white, shade 001 (C)
Pair each No. 6 and No. 10 knitting needles, use either extra long needles or circular needles

MEASUREMENTS
One size, to fit up to bust 42 in, 107 cm
Actual measurement – 63 in, 160 cm
Length – 26¾ in, 68 cm
Sleeve length – 14½ in, 37 cm

GAUGE
15 sts and 15 rows to 4 in (10 cm) over pat on No. 10 needles

ABBREVIATIONS
beg – beginning; cm – centimeters; cont – continue; dec – decrease; in – inches; inc – increase; k – knit; p – purl; pat – pattern, rem – remaining; rep – repeat; sl – slip; st(s) – stitch(es); st-st – stockinette stitch

NOTE
If using circular needles, work forwards and back in rows

NORTHERN LIGHTS

STAR GAZER

SWEATER
BACK
With No. 6 needles and B, cast on
121 sts.
Work 6 rows in k 1, p 1 rib, beg
wrong-side rows p 1.
Change to No. 10 needles.
P 1 row with A. P 1 row with C.
Cont in st-st from Chart 1 thus:
1st row (right side) Reading row 1 of
chart from right to left, k the 20 pat sts
6 times, then k last st of chart.
2nd row Reading row 2 of chart from
left to right, p first st of chart then p 20
pat sts 6 times.
3rd to 29th rows As 1st and 2nd rows
but working rows 3 to 29 of chart.
*Cont from Chart 2 thus:
1st row (wrong side) Reading row 1
of chart from left to right, p first st then
p 40 pat sts 3 times.
2nd row Reading row 2 of chart from
right to left, k the 40 pat sts 3 times,
then k last st of chart.
3rd to 34th rows As 1st and 2nd rows
but working rows 3 to 34 of chart**.
Rep from * to ** once.
Bind off with M.

FRONT
Work as back to **.
Cont from Chart 2 and work 1st to
28th rows again.

Neck Shaping
Next row Pat 47 sts, turn.
Keeping pat correct cont on these sts
only for 1st side and leave rem sts on a
spare needle.
Dec 1 st at neck edge on the next 5
rows.
Bind off rem 42 sts with M.
With right side facing, sl center 27 sts
on to a stitch holder, rejoin yarn to
inner end of rem 47 sts and complete
to match 1st side.

SLEEVES
With No. 6 needles and B, cast on
41 sts.
Work 6 rows in k 1, p 1 rib, beg
wrong-side rows p 1.
Change to No. 10 needles.
P 1 row with A. P 1 row with C.
Cont in st-st from Chart 1 thus:
1st row (right side) Reading row 1 of
chart from right to left, k the 20 pat sts
twice, then k last st of chart.
2nd row Reading row 2 of chart from
left to right, p first st of chart then p 20
pat sts twice.

3rd to 29th rows Increasing 1 st at
each end of every right-side row, work
as set on 1st and 2nd rows but working
rows 3 to 29 of chart, taking extra sts
into pat. 69 sts.
Cont from Chart 3 thus:
1st row (wrong side) Reading row 1
of chart from left to right, p first 3 sts of
chart then p 6 pat sts 11 times.
Cont from Chart 3 as set on 1st row,
reading right-side rows from right to
left and inc 1 st at each end of every
right-side row until there are 87 sts
and a total of 19 rows of Chart 3 have
been completed.
Next row K with B, inc 1 st at each end
of row.
Bind off the 89 sts with B.

NECKBAND
Join right shoulder seam.
With right side facing, using No. 10
needles and A, pick up and k 9 sts
down left front neck, k across 27 sts at
center front, pick up and k 8 sts up
right front neck then pick up and k 37
sts across center 37 sts of back, 81 sts.
Cont in st-st from Chart 1 thus:
Next row Reading row 25 of chart
from left to right, p first st of chart, then
p 20 pat sts 4 times.
Next row Reading row 26 of chart
from right to left, k 20 pat sts 4 times,
then k last st of chart.
Rep last 2 rows once but work rows
27 and 28 of chart.
P 1 row with A.
Change to No. 6 needles.
P 1 row with B. With B, work 5 rows in
p 1, k 1 rib, beg right-side rows k 1.
Bind off in rib.

FINISHING
Press. Join left shoulder and neckband
seam. With center of bind-off edge of

sleeves to shoulder seams, sew on
sleeves. Taking ½ st from each edge
into seams, join side and sleeve seams.

HAT
With No. 6 needles and B, cast on
81 sts.
Work 6 rows in k 1, p 1 rib, beg
wrong-side rows p 1.
Change to No. 10 needles.
P 1 row with A. P 1 row with C.
Cont in st-st from Chart 1 thus:
1st row (right side) Reading row 1 of
chart from right to left, k the 20 pat sts
4 times, then k last st of chart.
2nd row Reading row 2 of chart from
left to right, p first st of chart then p 20
pat sts 4 times.
3rd to 24th rows As 1st and 2nd rows
but working rows 3 to 24 of chart.
Bind off with A.

FINISHING
Press. Taking ½ st from each edge into
seam, join center back seam. With
seam to center, join bind-off edges.
With M, make 2 small tassels and
secure 1 to each end of top seam.

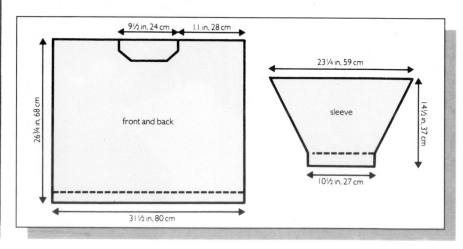

CHART 1

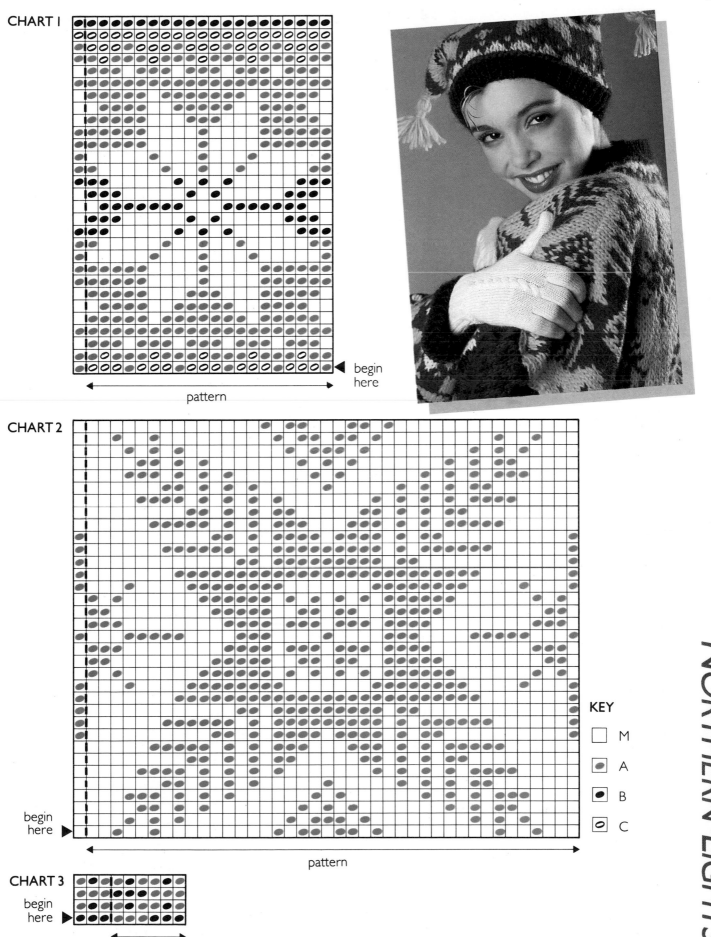

CHART 2

begin
here ◀

pattern

KEY

☐ M

◉ A

● B

⊘ C

CHART 3

begin
here ◀

pattern

NORTHERN LIGHTS

BROCADE

BROCADE

FINE ROMANCE

THE FABRIC IS A RICH MIXTURE OF MOHAIR AND METALLIC YARN, FALLING IN SOFT FOLDS. THE STYLE IS SIMPLE AND RELAXED ENOUGH TO WEAR WITH CASUAL CLOTHES. DESIGNED BY ZOE HUNT

MATERIALS
7 × 40 g balls Georges Picaud No 1 Kid Mohair shade 163 (M)
17 × 20 g balls Georges Picaud Feu d'Artifice shade 14 (A)
Pair each No. 4 and No. 6 knitting needles

MEASUREMENTS
One size, to fit up to bust 38 in, 97 cm
Actual measurement – 49 in, 125 cm
Length – 27 in, 69 cm
Sleeve length – 17¼ in, 44 cm

GAUGE
22 sts and 24 rows to 4 in (10 cm) measured over pat on No. 6 needles

ABBREVIATIONS
alt – alternate; beg – beginning; cm – centimeters; cont – continue; dec – decrease; foll – following; in – inches; inc – increas(e)(ing); k – knit; m 1 – make 1 st by picking up the strand between sts and k it through the back of the loop; p – purl; pat – pattern; rem – remaining; rep – repeat; st(s) – stitch(es); st-st – stockinette stitch

BACK
With No. 4 needles and M, cast on 120 sts.

Work in k 1, p 1 rib in stripes of 2 rows M, 4 rows A, 2 rows M, 4 rows A, 2 rows M, 4 rows A and 1 row M.
Next row With M, rib 3, m 1, *rib 6, m 1; rep from * to last 3 sts, rib 3. 140 sts.
Change to No. 6 needles.
Carrying color not in use loosely through every 3rd or 4th st on wrong side, cont in st-st from chart thus (noting that chart is in two halves, but should be read as one):
1st row (right side) Reading from right to left, k row 1 of chart.
2nd row Reading from left to right, p row 2 of chart.
Cont in this way until all 100 rows of chart have been worked (mark each end of row 82 to denote beg of armholes), then rep rows 1 to 50.

Shoulder and Neck Shaping
Cont from chart taking care to keep pat correct.
Bind off 16 sts at beg of next 2 rows.
Next row Bind off 15 sts, k until there are 27 sts on right needle, turn.
Cont on these sts only for 1st side and leave rem sts on a spare needle.
Bind off 12 sts at beg of next row.
Bind off rem 15 sts.
Next row With right side facing, bind off center 24 sts, pat to end.
Bind off 15 sts at beg of next row and 12 sts on the foll row.
Bind off rem 15 sts.

FRONT
Work as back until a total of 136 rows of pat have been worked.

Neck Shaping
1st row Pat 62 sts, turn.
Cont on these sts only for 1st side and leave rem sts on a spare needle.
Bind off 4 sts at beg of next row, 3 sts on the foll 2 alt rows and 2 sts on the next 2 alt rows. Dec 1 st at neck edge on the next 2 alt rows. 46 sts.

Shoulder Shaping
Bind off 16 sts at beg of next row and 15 sts on the foll alt row.
Pat 1 row. Bind off rem 15 sts.
Next row With right side facing, bind off center 16 sts, pat to end.

BROCADE

90
82

50

36

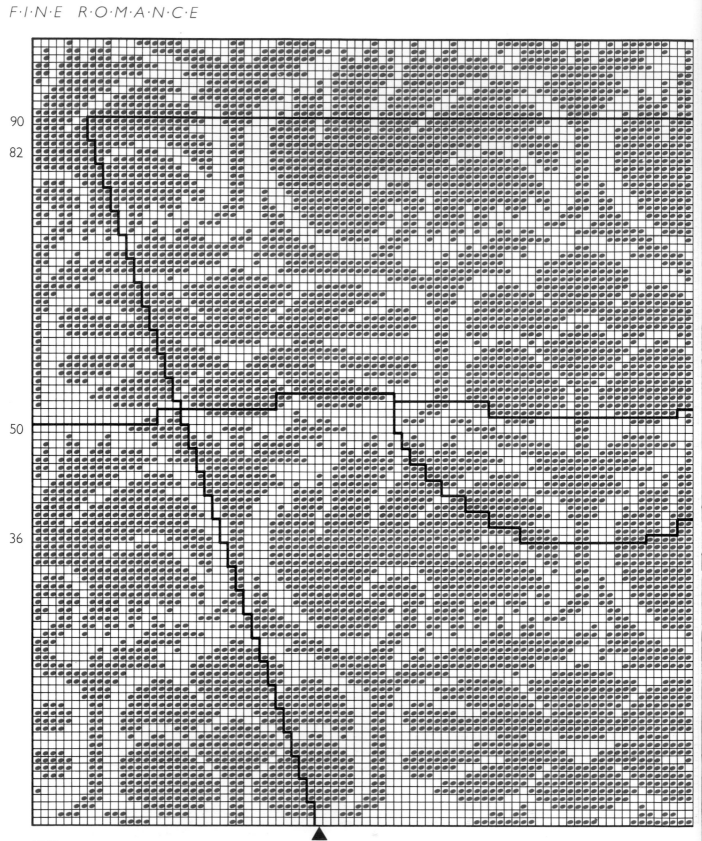

sleeve

KEY

☐ M

▣ A

90

82

50

36

▲
begin here for
sleeve

▲
begin here for
front and back

Pat 1 row.
Complete to match 1st side.

SLEEVES

With No. 4 needles and M, cast on
44 sts.
Rib 19 rows as back.
Next row With M, inc in first st, m 1,
*rib 2, m 1; rep from * to last st, inc in
last st. 68 sts.
Change to No. 6 needles.
Working sts indicated, cont from chart,
inc 1 st at each end of 4th row and
every foll 3rd row until there are 126
sts.
Pat 2 rows straight, thus ending with
row 90. Bind off loosely.

NECKBAND

Join right shoulder seam.
With right side facing, using No. 4
needles and M, pick up and k 70 sts
evenly around front neck and 50 sts
around back neck. 120 sts.
K 1 row.
Bind off knit-wise.

FINISHING

Press pieces lightly on wrong side using
a cool iron. Join left shoulder and
neckband seam. With center of bind-
off edge of sleeves to shoulder seams,
sew on sleeves. Join side and sleeve
seams.

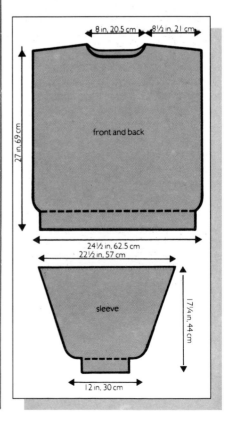

8 in, 20.5 cm   8½ in, 21 cm

27 in, 69 cm

front and back

24½ in, 62.5 cm
22½ in, 57 cm

17¼ in, 44 cm

sleeve

12 in, 30 cm

FINE ROMANCE

STREET SMART

STREET SMART

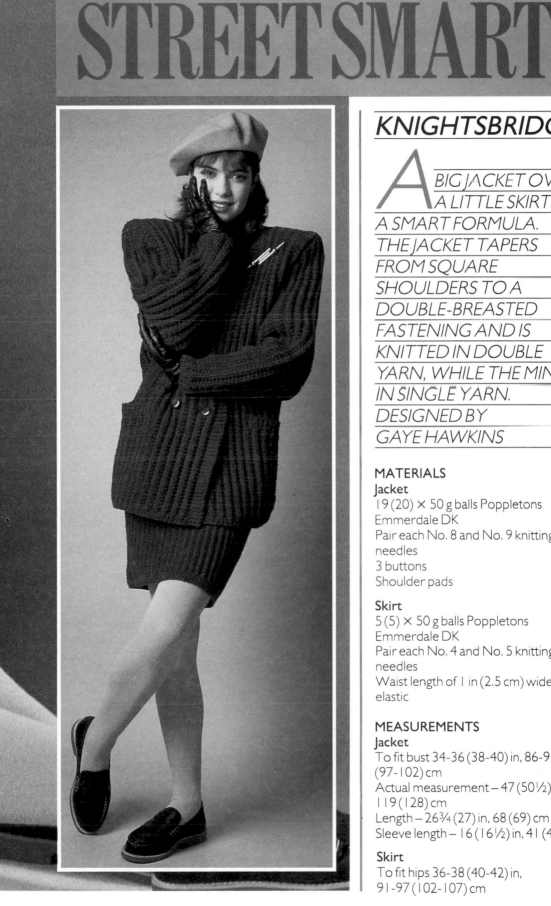

KNIGHTSBRIDGE

A BIG JACKET OVER A LITTLE SKIRT IS A SMART FORMULA. THE JACKET TAPERS FROM SQUARE SHOULDERS TO A DOUBLE-BREASTED FASTENING AND IS KNITTED IN DOUBLE YARN, WHILE THE MINI IS IN SINGLE YARN. DESIGNED BY GAYE HAWKINS

MATERIALS
Jacket
19 (20) × 50 g balls Poppletons
Emmerdale DK
Pair each No. 8 and No. 9 knitting
needles
3 buttons
Shoulder pads

Skirt
5 (5) × 50 g balls Poppletons
Emmerdale DK
Pair each No. 4 and No. 5 knitting
needles
Waist length of 1 in (2.5 cm) wide
elastic

MEASUREMENTS
Jacket
To fit bust 34-36 (38-40) in, 86-91
(97-102) cm
Actual measurement – 47 (50½) in,
119 (128) cm
Length – 26¾ (27) in, 68 (69) cm
Sleeve length – 16 (16½) in, 41 (42) cm

Skirt
To fit hips 36-38 (40-42) in,
91-97 (102-107) cm

K·N·I·G·H·T·S·B·R·I·D·G·E

Actual measurement – 36½ (39) in, 93 (99) cm
Length – 19¼, 49 cm
Figures in parenthesis are for larger size

GAUGE
Jacket
17 sts and 24 rows to 4 in (10 cm) over pat on No. 9 needles using 2 strands of yarn

Skirt
26 sts and 32 rows to 4 in (10 cm) over pat on No. 5 needles using 1 strand of yarn

ABBREVIATIONS
alt – alternate; beg – beginning; cm – centimeters; cont – continue; dec – decrease; foll – following; g-st – garter stitch; in – inches; inc – increase; k – knit; p – purl; pat – pattern; rem – remain(ing); rep – repeat; sl – slip; st(s) – stitch(es); st-st – stockinette stitch; tog – together

JACKET
BACK
With No. 8 needles and 2 strands of yarn, cast on 93 (101) sts.
1st rib row (right side) K 1, *p 1, k 1; rep from * to end.
2nd rib row P 1, *k 1, p 1; rep from * to end.
Rep 1st and 2nd rib rows once.
Change to No. 9 needles.
Cont in pat thus:
1st row (right side) P 1, *k 3, p 1; rep from * to end.
2nd row K 2, *p 1, k 3; rep from * to last 3 sts, p 1, k 2.
These 2 rows form pat for back.
Cont in pat inc 1 st at each end of every 16th row until there are 103 (111) sts, working inc sts into pat.
Pat 12 rows straight.

Armhole Shaping
Keeping pat correct, bind off 8 sts at beg of next 2 rows. Dec 1 st at each end of every right-side row until 77 (85) sts rem.
Pat 55 (57) rows straight.

Shoulder Shaping
Bind off 11 (13) sts at beg of next 4 rows. Bind off rem 33 sts.

POCKET LININGS
Make 2 With No. 9 needles and 1 strand of yarn, cast on 23 sts.
Work in st-st for 8¼ in (21 cm), ending

with a p row.
Break off yarn and leave sts on a stitch holder.

LEFT FRONT
With No. 8 needles and 2 strands of yarn, cast on 66 (70) sts.
1st rib row (right side) *K 1, p 1; rep from * to last 6 sts, k 6.
2nd rib row K 5, *p1, k 1; rep from * to last st, p 1.
Rep 1st and 2nd rib rows once.
Change to No. 9 needles.
Cont in pat thus:
1st row (right side) *P 1, k 3; rep from * to last 6 sts, p 1, k 5.
2nd row K 7, *p 1, k 3; rep from * to last 3 sts, p 1, k 2.
These 2 rows form pat for left front.
Cont in pat inc 1 st at end of every

16th row until there are 69 (73) sts, working inc sts into pat.
Pat 2 rows straight, thus ending with a 2nd row.
Pocket Opening row Pat 6 (10) sts, sl next 23 sts on to a stitch holder, pat across sts of one pocket lining, pat 40.
Pat 7 rows straight.
1st buttonhole row (right side) Pat 57 (61) sts, bind off next 4, pat to end.
2nd buttonhole row Pat 8, cast on 4 sts, pat to end.
Pat 3 rows straight.
Inc 1 st at end of next row.

Front Shaping
1st row (right side) Pat to last 7 sts, k 2 tog, k 5.
Pat 2 rows.

4th row K 5, k 2 tog, pat to end.
Pat 2 rows.
Inc I st at end of 16th row from previous inc, AND AT THE SAME TIME, rep last 6 rows until 61 (65) sts rem, ending with a 4th row.

Armhole Shaping
Bind off 8 sts at beg of next row, then dec I st at armhole edge on the next 5 right-side rows, AND AT THE SAME TIME, dec at front edge as before until 27 (31) sts rem.
Pat 3 (5) rows straight, thus ending at armhole edge.

Shoulder Shaping
Bind off 11 (13) sts at beg of next row and on the foll alt row.
Work 3¾ in (9.5 cm) in g-st on rem 5 st. Bind off.

RIGHT FRONT
With No. 8 needles and 2 strands of yarn, cast on 66 (70) sts.
1st rib row (right side) K 6, *p I, k I; rep from * to end.
2nd rib row *P I, k I; rep from * to last 6 sts, p I, k 5.
Rep 1st and 2nd rib rows once.
Change to No. 9 needles.
Cont in pat thus:
1st row (right side) K 5, p I, *k 3, p I; rep from * to end.
2nd row K 2, p I, *k 3, p I; rep from * to last 7 sts, k 7.
These 2 rows form pat for right front.
Cont in pat inc I st at beg of every 16th row until there are 69 (73) sts, working inc sts into pat.
Pat 2 rows straight, thus ending with a 2nd row.
Pocket Opening row Pat 40, sl next 23 sts on to a stitch holder, pat across sts of pocket lining, pat 6 (10).
Pat 7 rows straight.
1st buttonhole row (right side) Pat 8, bind off next 4 sts, pat to end.
2nd buttonhole row Pat 57 (61) sts, cast on 4 sts, pat to end.
Pat 3 rows straight.
Inc I st at beg of next row.

Front Shaping
1st row (right side) K 5, k 2 tog, pat to end.
Pat 2 rows.
4th row Pat to last 7 sts, k 2 tog, k 5.
Pat 2 rows.
Inc I st at beg of 16th row from previous inc, AND AT THE SAME

TIME, rep last 6 rows until 61 (65) sts rem, ending with a 4th row.
Pat 1 row.
Complete to match left front from armhole shaping but pat 1 extra row before working shoulder shaping.

SLEEVES
With No. 8 needles and 2 strands of yarn, cast on 45 (49) sts.
Rib 4 rows as given at beg of back.
Change to No. 9 needles.
Cont in pat thus:
1st row (right side) K 0 (2), *p I, k 3; rep from * to last I (3) sts, p I, k0 (2).
This row sets pat.
Working inc sts into pat to match back, *pat 2 rows, inc I st at each end of next row, pat 3 rows, inc I st at each end of next row*. Rep from * to * until there are 97 (101) sts.
Pat 2 (4) rows straight.

Cap Shaping
Bind off 8 sts at beg of next 2 rows.
Dec I st at each end of next row and every foll alt row until 71 (75) sts rem, then on every row until 23 (27) sts rem. Bind off.

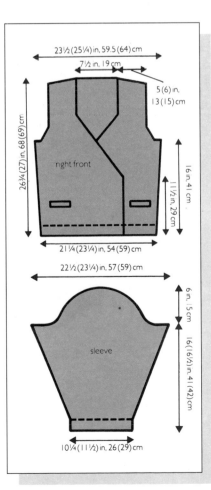

POCKET TOPS
With right side facing, using No. 8 needles and 2 strands of yarn, work 4 rows in p I, k I rib across sts on stitch holder. Bind off in rib.

FINISHING
Sew down pocket linings on wrong side and sides of pocket tops on right side. Join shoulder seams. Join bind-off edges of back neckbands then sew to back neck. Join side and sleeve seams. Set in sleeves. Sew I button to right side of left front to correspond to right front buttonhole. Sew I button to wrong side of right front to correspond to left front buttonhole. Sew rem button to right side of right front in the same position as button on wrong side. Sew in shoulder pads.

SKIRT

BACK AND FRONT ALIKE
With No. 4 needles and I strand of yarn, cast on 123 (131) sts.
1st rib row (right side) P I, *k I, p I; rep from * to end.
2nd rib row K I, *p I, k I; rep from * to end.
Rep 1st and 2nd rib rows 3 times.
Change to No. 5 needles.
Cont in pat thus:
1st row (right side) K 3, *p I, k 3; rep from * to end.
2nd row K I, *p I, k 3; rep from * to last 2 sts, p I, k I.
These 2 rows form pat.
Rep these 2 rows until work measures 11 in (28 cm) from cast-on edge, ending with a 2nd row.

Hip Shaping
Keeping pat correct, dec I st at each end of next row and every foll 4th row until 91 (99) sts rem. Pat 3 rows straight.
Change to No. 4 needles. Rep 1st and 2nd rib rows 5 times. Bind off in rib.

FINISHING
Join side seams. Join elastic into ring and attach to wrong side of waist rib using a herringbone casing.

STREET SMART

KENSINGTON

THERE'S AN ESSENTIALLY ENGLISH FEEL ABOUT A LONG SWEATER OVER AN EVEN LONGER SKIRT. DOUBLE RIBS AND CONTRAST EDGINGS ARE DISTINCTIVE FEATURES. DESIGNED BY BRENDA SPARKES

MATERIALS
Sweater
14 × 50 g balls Patons Beehive Double Knitting (A)
1 × 50 g ball Patons Beehive Double Knitting (B)
Pair each No. 2 and No. 4 knitting needles
No. 2 circular knitting needle – 36 in (100 cm) long
Cable needle

Skirt
9 × 50 g balls Patons Beehive Double Knitting (A)
1 × 50 g ball Patons Beehive Double Knitting (B)
Pair each No. 3 and No. 4 knitting needles
Waist length of 1 in (2.5 cm) wide elastic

MEASUREMENTS
Sweater
One size, to fit up to bust 36 in, 91 cm
Actual measurement – 44 in, 112 cm
Length – 30¾ in, 78 cm
Sleeve length – 18 in, 46 cm

Skirt
One size, to fit up to hips 38 in, 97 cm
Length – 33½ in, 85 cm

GAUGE
Sweater
36 sts (1 pat rep) to 4½ in (11.5 cm) and 30 rows to 4 in (10 cm) over pat on No. 4 needles

Skirt
26 st to 4 in (10 cm) measured over slightly stretched rib on No. 4 needles

K·E·N·S·I·N·G·T·O·N

ABBREVIATIONS

beg – beginning; c12 – slip next 6 sts on to cable needle and hold at front, k 6 then k 6 from cable needle; cm – centimeters; cont – continue; dec – decrease; in – inches; inc – increase(ing); k – knit; p – purl; pat – pattern; rem – remain(ing); rep – repeat; st(s) – stitch(es); tog – together

SWEATER
BACK

First Rib With No. 2 needles and B, cast on 120 sts.
Work 1 row in k 2, p 2 rib.
Change to A and cont in k 2, p 2 rib for 2½ in (6 cm).
Change to B and rib 1 row.
Break yarn and leave sts on a spare needle.
Second rib Work as for first rib but cont in A for 5½ in (14 cm), then change to B and rib 1 row. Do not break yarn.
Joining row Place first rib in front of second rib and with B rib to end working 1 st from each needle tog. 120 sts.
Cont in A.
Inc row P 2, *inc in next st, p 1; rep from * to last 2 sts, p 2. 178 sts.
Change to No. 4 needles.
Cont in pat thus:

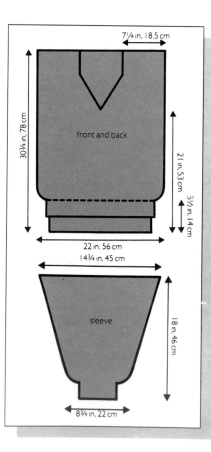

7¼ in, 18.5 cm

front and back

30¾ in, 78 cm

21 in, 53 cm

5½ in, 14 cm

22 in, 56 cm

14¾ in, 45 cm

sleeve

18 in, 46 cm

8¾ in, 22 cm

1st row (right side) P 2, k 2, *p 1, k 24, p 1, k 2, p 2, k 2, p 2, k 2; rep from * to last 30 sts, p 1, k 24, p 1, k 2, p 2.
2nd row K 2, p 2, *k 2, p 22, k 2, p 2, k 2, p 2, k 2, p 2; rep from * to last 30 sts, k 2, p 22, k 2, p 2, k 2.
3rd row P 2, k 2, *p 3, k 20, p 3, k 2, p 2, k 2, p 2, k 2; rep from * to last 30 sts, p 3, k 20, p 3, k 2, p 2.
4th row K 2, p 2, *k 4, p 18, k 4, p 2, k 2, p 2, k 2, p 2; rep from * to last 30 sts, k 4, p 18, k 4, p 2, k 2.
5th row P 2, k 2, *p 5, k 2, c 12, k 2, p 5, k 2, p 2, k 2, p 2, k 2; rep from * to last 30 sts, p 5, k 2, c 12, k 2, p 5, k 2, p 2.
6th row K 2, p 2, *k 6, p 14, k 6, p 2, k 2, p 2, k 2, p 2; rep from * to last 30 sts, k 6, p 14, k 6, p 2, k 2.
7th row P 2, k 2, *p 5, k 16, p 5, k 2, p 2, k 2, p 2, k 2; rep from * to last 30 sts, p 5, k 16, p 5, k 2, p 2.
8th row As 4th row.
9th row As 3rd row.
10th row As 2nd row.
These 10 rows form pat.
Pat straight until back measures 30¾ in (78 cm) from cast-on edge of second rib. Bind off.

FRONT

Work as back until front measures 21 in (53 cm) from cast-on edge of second rib, ending with a wrong-side row.

Neck Shaping

1st row Pat 89 sts, turn.
Keeping pat correct, cont on these sts only for 1st side and leave rem sts on a spare needle.
Dec 1 st at neck edge on every right-side row until 58 sts rem.
Pat straight until front matches back to shoulder. Bind off.
Next row With right side facng, rejoin A to inner end of 89 sts on spare needle and pat to end.
Complete to match 1st side.

SLEEVES

With No. 2 needles and B, cast on 56 sts.
Work 1 row in k 2, p 2 rib.
Change to A and cont in rib until sleeve measures 3 in (8 cm) from cast-on edge.
Change to B and rib 1 row.
Inc row *P 3, inc in next st; rep from * to end. 70 sts.
Change to No. 4 needles and cont in A.
Work in pat as back, inc 1 st at each end of every 3rd row until there are

142 sts, working inc sts in k 2, p 2 rib.
Pat straight until sleeve measures 18 in (46 cm) from cast-on edge.
Bind off loosely.

NECKBAND

Matching sts, join both shoulder seams.
With right side facing, using No. 2 circular needle and B and beg at center. front, pick up and k 92 sts evenly up right front neck, 48 sts across back neck and 92 sts down left front neck. 232 sts.
Work forwards and back in rows.
Work 1 row in k 2, p 2 rib.
Twisting A and B tog on wrong side to prevent holes, cont thus:
Next row (right side) K 1 with B, rib to end with A.
Next row With A, rib to last st, p 1 with B.
Rep last 2 rows 4 times.
Rib 1 row with B.
Bind off in rib with B.

FINISHING

With center of bind-off edge of sleeves to shoulder seams, sew on sleeves.
Join sleeve seams. Joining the two ribs separately, join side seams.
Overlap B end of neckband over other end and sew row-ends neatly to sides of 'V'.

SKIRT
BACK

With No. 4 needles and B, cast on 142 sts.
1st rib row (right side) K 2, *p 2, k 2; rep from * to end.
Cont in A.
2nd rib row P 2, *k 2, p 2; rep from * to end.
Rep last 2 rows until work measures 33½ in (85 cm) from cast-on edge, ending with a wrong-side row.
Change to No. 3 needles.
Rib 10 rows.
Bind off loosely in rib.

FRONT

Work as for back.

FINISHING

Join side seams. Join elastic into ring and attach to wrong side of waist rib using a herringbone casing.

BELGRAVIA

MORE THAN A
LONG SWEATER
– THIS DRESS FORMS A
SLEEK WEDGE,
WIDENING OUT INTO
BIG SHOULDERS WITH
UNUSUAL RAGLAN
AND SADDLE SHAPING.
DESIGNED BY
BRENDA SPARKES

MATERIALS
2 (3, 3) × 500 g cones Rowan Light
Weight DK
Pair each No. 3 and No. 5 knitting
needles
No. 2 circular knitting needle,
16 in (40 cm) long
Raglan shoulder pads

MEASUREMENTS
To fit bust 34 (36, 38) in, 86 (91, 97) cm
Actual measurement – 44½ (47,
49) in, 113 (119, 125) cm
Length – 36½ (37½, 38½) in, 93
(95, 97) cm
Sleeve length – 16 (16½, 17) in, 41
(42, 43) cm
Figures in parenthesis are for larger
sizes

GAUGE
25 sts and 42 rows to 4 in (10 cm)
measured over pat on No. 5 needles

ABBREVIATIONS
beg – beginning; cm – centimeters;
cont – continue; dec – decrease; fol –
following; in – inches; inc –
increas(ed)(ing); k – knit; p – purl; pat –
pattern; rem – remain(ing); rep –
repeat; sl – slip; sl 1 p – slip 1 stitch
purlwise; st(s) – stitch(es); tbl – through
back of loop(s); tog – together; yo –
yarn over

BACK
With No. 3 needles, cast on 105 (113,
121) sts.
1st rib row (right side) K 2, *p 1, k 1;
rep from * to last st, k 1.
2nd rib row K 1, *p 1, k 1; rep from *
to end.
Rep 1st and 2nd rib row for ¾ in (2 cm),
ending with a 2nd rib row.
Change to No. 5 needles.

STREET SMART

Cont in pat thus:
1st row (right side) K 2, *yo, sl 1 p, leave yarn at front, k 1; rep from * to last st, k 1.
2nd row K 1, *p 1, k the slipped st and the made st tog; rep from * to last 2 sts, p 1, k 1.
These 2 rows form pat.
Cont in pat, inc 1 st at each end of 15th row and every foll 14th row until there are 141 (149, 157) sts, working inc sts into pat.
Pat straight until work measures 26 in (66 cm) from cast-on edge, ending with a wrong-side row.

Raglan Shaping
Dec 1 st at each end of every right-side row until 47 sts rem, ending with a wrong-side row.
Bind off loosely.

FRONT
Work as back until 61 sts rem, ending with a wrong-side row.

Neck Shaping
1st row K 2 tog, pat 18 sts, turn.
Cont on these 19 sts only for 1st side and leave rem sts on a spare needle.
Keeping pat correct, cont to dec at raglan edge on every right-side row, AND AT THE SAME TIME, dec 1 st at neck edge on the next 11 rows. 3 sts.
Dec 1 st at raglan edge on the next

row. Pat 1 row.
K 2 tog and fasten off.
Next row With right side facing, sl center 21 sts on to a stitch holder, rejoin yarn to inner end of rem 20 sts, pat 18, K 2 tog.
Complete to match 1st side.

LEFT SLEEVE
With No. 3 needles, cast on 51 (55, 59) sts.
Rib 3 in (8 cm) as given at beg of back, ending with a 2nd rib row.
Change to No. 5 needles.
Cont in pat, inc 1 st at each end of every 4th row until there are 105 (107, 109) sts, then on every foll 3rd row until there are 119 (127, 135) sts, working inc sts into pat.
Pat straight until sleeve measures 16 (16½, 17) in, 41 (42, 43) cm from cast-on edge, ending with a wrong-side row.

Raglan Shaping
1st row Rib 46 (50, 54), k 2 tog, rib 23, k 2 tog tbl, rib 46 (50, 54).
2nd row Pat to end.
3rd row Rib 45 (49, 53), k 2 tog, rib 23, k 2 tog tbl, rib 45 (49, 53).
4th row As 2nd.
5th row Rib 44 (48, 52), k 2 tog, rib 23, k 2 tog tbl, rib 44 (48, 52).
Cont to dec in this way, keeping center 27 sts as set and working 1 st less at each end on every successive right-side row until 25 sts rem, ending with a wrong-side row.

Saddle Shaping
1st row Pat 13 sts, turn.
Cont on these sts only for saddle extension and leave rem 12 sts on a safety pin.
Work in pat for 3¾ in (9.5 cm), ending with a wrong-side row.
Bind off loosely.

RIGHT SLEEVE
Work to match left sleeve but end with a right-side row before working saddle shaping.

COLLAR
Join raglan seams. Join bind-off edges of saddle extensions at top of sleeves. Join saddle extensions to bind-off sts at top of back. Join side and sleeve seams.
Note on 1st row of collar, when working across sts on safety pin on right sleeve, p the slipped st and the made st tog each time.
1st row With right side facing and using No. 2 circular knitting needle, pick up and k 27 sts across right saddle extension and 28 sts across left saddle extension, work in p 1, k 1 rib across sts on safety pin, pick up and k 18 sts evenly down left front neck, work in p 1, k 1 rib across sts at center front, pick up and k 18 sts up right front neck, work in k 1, p 1 rib across sts on safety pin. 136 sts.
Work in rounds of k 1, p 1 rib for 5½ in (14 cm). Bind off loosely in rib.
Sew in shoulder pads.

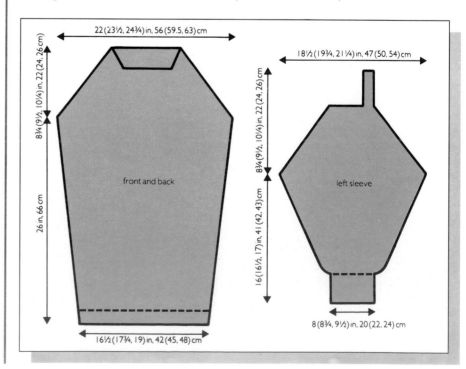

front and back

22 (23½, 24¾) in, 56 (59.5, 63) cm

8¾ (9½, 10¼) in, 22 (24, 26) cm

26 in, 66 cm

16½ (17¾, 19) in, 42 (45, 48) cm

left sleeve

18½ (19¾, 21¼) in, 47 (50, 54) cm

8¾ (9½, 10¼) in, 22 (24, 26) cm

16 (16½, 17) in, 41 (42, 43) cm

8 (8¾, 9½) in, 20 (22, 24) cm

SKI GRAPHIQUE

SKI GRAPHIQUE

SUPERSAMPLER

SWEATER, HOOD AND COWL ADD UP TO A MONTAGE OF CRISP CONTRASTING AND COMPLEMENTARY PATTERNS. THE GRAPHICS AND SIZING WOULD MAKE IT A GREAT SWEATER FOR A MAN, TOO. DESIGNED BY MARY NORDEN

MATERIALS
Wendy Shetland Double Knit
Sweater
6 × 50 g balls Tiree (M)
4 × 50 g balls Rhum (A)
3 × 50 g balls Othello (B)
2 × 50 g balls Barra (C)
2 × 50 g balls White Heather (D)
Cowl
2 × 50 g balls Othello (B)
2 × 50 g balls White Heather (D)
Hood
2 × 50 g balls White Heather (D)
2 × 50 g balls Herma Ness (E)
Pair each No. 2 and No. 4 knitting
needles for sweater and hood
No. 6 circular knitting needle,
24 in (60 cm) long for cowl

MEASUREMENTS
Sweater
To fit up to bust 42 in, 107 cm
Actual measurement – 46½ in, 118 cm
approx
Length – 28 in, 71 cm approx
Sleeve length – 18½ in, 47 cm approx
Cowl
Length – 21¼ in, 54 cm
Hood
Length – 23 in, 58 cm

GAUGE
26 sts and 26 rows to 4 in (10 cm) over
st-st Fair Isle on No. 4 needles
22 sts and 30 rows to 4 in (10 cm) over
st-st on No. 6 needles

ABBREVIATIONS
alt – alternate; beg – beginning; cm –

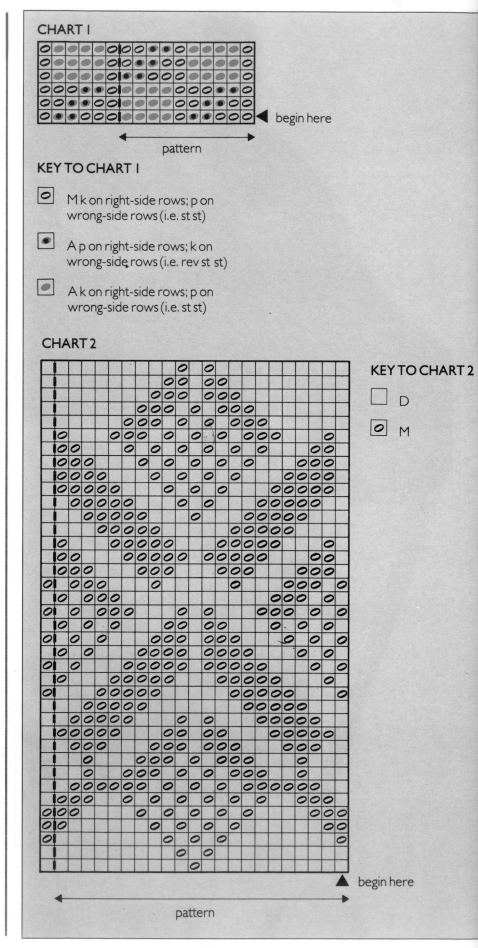

CHART 1

pattern ◀ begin here

KEY TO CHART 1

⊙ M k on right-side rows; p on wrong-side rows (i.e. st st)

● A p on right-side rows; k on wrong-side rows (i.e. rev st st)

◐ A k on right-side rows; p on wrong-side rows (i.e. st st)

CHART 2

KEY TO CHART 2

☐ D

⊙ M

▲ begin here

pattern

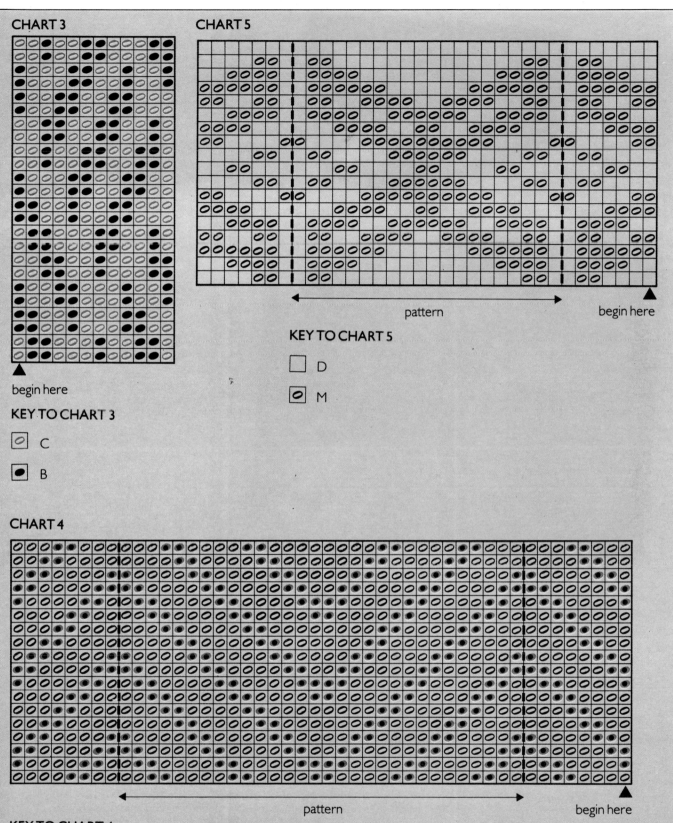

CHART 3

begin here

KEY TO CHART 3

⌀	C
⬤	B

CHART 5

pattern

begin here

KEY TO CHART 5

☐	D
⌀	M

CHART 4

pattern

begin here

KEY TO CHART 4

⬤	A p on right-side rows; k on wrong-side rows (i.e. rev st st)
⌀	M k on right-side rows; p on wrong-side rows (i.e. st st)

SKI GRAPHIQUE

centimeters; cont – continue; dec – decrease; foll – following; in – inches; inc – increase; k – knit; p – purl; pat – pattern; rem – remaining; rep – repeat; st(s) – stitch(es); st-st – stockinette stitch

BACK

With No. 2 needles and M, cast on 156 sts.
Work 1¼ in (3 cm) in k 1, p 1 rib.
Change to No. 4 needles.
Cont from Chart 1 thus:
1st row (right side) Reading row 1 of chart from right to left, work 10 pat sts 15 times, then work last 6 sts of chart.
2nd row Reading row 2 of chart from left to right, work first 6 sts of chart, then work 10 pat sts 15 times.
3rd to 6th rows As 1st and 2nd rows but working rows 3 to 6 of chart.
Rep 1st to 6th rows until work measures approx 13¾ in (35 cm) from

cast-on edge, ending with a 6th row.
K 1 row B. P 1 row D. Rep from * to * twice, dec 1 st at end of last row. 155 sts.
Cont in st-st from Chart 2 thus:
1st row (right side) Reading row 1 of chart from right to left, k 22 pat sts 7 times, then k last st of chart.
2nd row Reading row 2 of chart from left to right, p first st of chart, then p 22 pat sts 7 times.
3rd to 38th rows As 1st and 2nd rows but working rows 3 to 38 of chart.
Inc 1 st at beg of 1st row, work from * to * twice, then k 1 row B. 156 sts.
Cont in st-st from Chart 3 thus:
1st row (wrong side) Reading row 1 of chart from left to right, p 12 sts of chart 13 times.
2nd row Reading row 2 of chart from right to left, k 12 sts of chart 13 times.
3rd to 24th rows As 1st and 2nd rows but working rows 3 to 24 of chart **.

Rep 1st to 15th rows of Chart 3.

Neck Shaping
Next row (right side) Working as row 16 of Chart 3, pat 66, bind off next 24 sts, pat to end.
Keeping pat correct, cont on last set of 66 sts only for 1st side and leave rem sts on a spare needle. Pat 1 row.
***Bind off 6 sts at beg of next row and on the foll alt row. Pat 1 row.
Bind off rem 54 sts.
With wrong side facing, rejoin yarn to inner end of 66 sts on spare needle and complete to match 1st side from *** but pat 2 rows not 1 before binding off.

FRONT

Work as back to **.
Rep 1st to 5th rows of Chart 3.

Neck Shaping
Next row (right side) Working as row 6 of Chart 3, pat 69, bind off next 18 sts, pat to end.
Keeping pat correct, cont on last set of 69 sts only for 1st side and leave rem sts on a spare needle. Pat 1 row.
****Bind off 5 sts at beg of next row, 3 sts on the foll alt row and 2 sts on the next 2 alt rows. Dec 1 st at beg of next 3 alt rows. Pat 1 row.
Bind off rem 54 sts.
With wrong side facing, rejoin yarn to inner end of sts on spare needle and complete to match 1st side from **** but pat 2 rows not 1 before binding off.

SLEEVES

With No. 2 needles and M, cast on 64 sts.
Work 2¾ in (7 cm) in k 1, p 1 rib.
Inc row Rib 4, *inc in next st, rib 4; rep from * to end. 76 sts.
Change to No. 4 needles.
Note When increasing always take increased sts into pat.
Cont from Chart 4 thus:
1st row (right side) Reading row 1 of chart from right to left, pat first 8 sts of chart, work 30 pat sts twice, then pat last 8 sts of chart.
2nd row Reading row 2 of chart from left to right, pat first 8 sts of chart, work 30 pat sts twice, then pat last 8 sts of chart. Beg with row 3, cont from chart in this way, inc 1 st at each end of next row and every foll 3rd row until there are 108 sts, thus ending with row

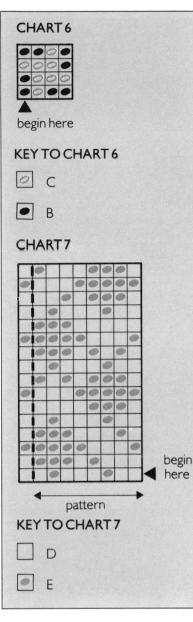

CHART 6

begin here

KEY TO CHART 6

| $\oslash$ | C |
| $\bullet$ | B |

CHART 7

begin here

pattern

KEY TO CHART 7

| $\square$ | D |
| $\boxdot$ | E |

12 of chart.
Work from * to * of back 3 times, but inc 1 st at each end of every p row. 114 sts.
Cont in st-st from Chart 5 thus:
1st row (right side) Reading row 1 of chart from right to left, k first 7 sts of chart, k 20 pat sts 5 times, then k last 7 sts of chart.
Work rows 2 to 18 of chart in this way, inc 1 st at each end of every p row. 132 sts. K 1 row B.
Next row With D, inc in first st, p to last st, inc in last st.
Rep last 2 rows once, then k 1 row B. 136 sts.
Cont in st-st from Chart 6 thus:
1st row (wrong side) With B, inc in first st, p 1 B, reading row 1 of chart from left to right, p 4 sts of chart to last 2 sts, p 1 B, with C inc in last st.

2nd row K 2 C, 1 B, reading row 2 of chart from right to left, k 4 sts of chart to last 3 sts, k 3 C.
3rd row With C inc in first st, k 1 C, k 1 B, reading row 3 of chart from left to right, p 4 sts of chart to last 3 sts, p 2 C, with C inc in last st.
4th row Reading row 4 of chart from right to left, k 4 sts of chart to end. Cont to inc on every p row in this way until there are 164 sts. Pat 1 row, thus ending with row 4 or chart. Bind off loosely.

NECKBAND
Join right shoulder seam.
With right side facing, using No. 2 needles and M, pick up and K 62 sts evenly around front neck and 56 sts around back neck. 118 sts.
Work 15 rows in k 1, p 1 rib.
Bind off loosely in rib.

FINISHING
Press. Join left shoulder and neckband seam. Fold neckband in half on to wrong side and whipstitch loosely in place. With center of bind-off edge of sleeves to shoulder seams, sew on sleeves. Join side and sleeve seams.

COWL
With No. 6 circular needle and B, cast on 146 sts.
Work throughout in stripes of 1 row D and 1 row B.
Rib 4 rounds.
Cont in st-st (every round k) until work measures 20½ in (52 cm) from cast-on edge, ending with 1 round in B.
Rib 4 rounds.
Bind off in rib with D.

HOOD
With No.2 needles and D, cast on 153 sts.
Work 2¾ in (7 cm) in k 1, p 1 rib, beg alt rows p 1.
Change to No.4 needles.
Cont in st-st from Chart 7 thus:
1st row (right side) Reading row 1 of chart from right to left, k 8 pat sts to last st, then k last st of chart.
2nd row Reading row 2 of chart from left to right, p first st of chart, then p 8 pat sts to end.
3rd to 16th rows As 1st and 2nd rows but working rows 3 to 16 of chart.
Rep 1st to 16th rows 7 times.
Change to No. 2 needles.
With E, rib 5 rows.
Bind off in rib with E.
Join seam.

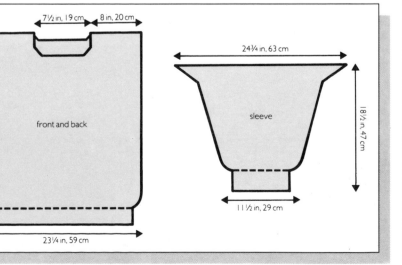

CAFE SOCIETY

CRIMSON

CAFE SOCIETY

CRIMSON

WHEN AN
OTHERWISE
SPORTY STYLE IS
KNITTED IN HEAVY,
SHINY, VISCOSE RIBBON
THE RESULT IS A
DAZZLING EVENING
TRANSFORMATION.
DESIGNED BY
KATE JONES

MATERIALS
21 × 50 g balls Pingouin Ruban
Pair each No. 8, No. 10½ and No. 11
knitting needles
Cable needle

MEASUREMENTS
One size, to fit up to bust 38 in, 97 cm
Actual measurement – 49½ in,
126 cm approx
Length – 24 in, 60 cm
Sleeve length – 16 in, 41 cm

GAUGE
13 sts and 17 rows to 4 in (10 cm)
measured over st-st on No. 11 needles

NOTE
In wear, gauge of garment may differ,
thus measurements may vary slightly
from those above

ABBREVIATIONS
alt – alternate; approx – approximate;
beg – beginning; c 3 b – sl next st on to
cable needle and hold at back, k 2 then
k 1 from cable needle; c 3 f – sl next 2
sts on to cable needle and hold at front,
k 1 then k 2 from cable needle; cm –
centimeters; cont – continue; foll –
following; g-st – garter stitch; in –
inches; inc – increase; k – knit; k 1 b –

knit into st 1 row below next st on left
needle and allow st above to drop off
needle; p – purl; pat – pattern; rem –
remaining; rep – repeat; sl – slip; st(s) –
stitch(es); st-st – stockinette stitch
Work instructions in square brackets
the number of times given

BACK
With No. 10½ needles, cast on 85 sts.
Work 4 rows in g-st.
Change to No. 11 needles.
Cont in zig-zag pat thus:
1st row (right side) K.
2nd and every foll alt row P.

3rd row K 33, [c 3 f, k 3] twice, c 3 f,
k 37.
5th row K 34, [c 3 f, k 3] twice, c 3 f,
k 36.
7th row K 35, [c 3 f, k 3] twice, c 3 f,
k 35.
9th row K 36, [c 3 f, k 3] twice, c 3 f,
k 34.
11th row K 37, [c 3 f, k 3] twice, c 3 f,
k 33.
13th row K.
15th row K 37, [c 3 b, k 3] twice, c 3 b,
k 33.
17th row K 36, [c 3 b, k 3] twice, c 3 b,
k 34.

19th row K 35, [c 3 b, k 3] twice, c 3 b, k 35.

21st row K 34, [c 3 b, k 3] twice, c 3 b, k 36.

23rd row K 33, [c 3 b, k 3] twice, c 3 b, k 37.

24th row P.

These 24 rows form pat.

Rep 1st to 24th rows twice, then work 1st to 16th rows again.

Neck Shaping

1st row (right side) K 36, bind off next 13 sts, k to end.

Cont in st-st on last set of 36 sts for 1st side. Leave rem sts on a spare needle. P 1 row.

** Bind off 4 sts at beg of next row, 2 sts on the foll 2 alt rows and 1 st on the next alt row. 27 sts. Work 2 rows straight. Bind off loosely.

Next row With wrong side facing, rejoin yarn to inner end of 36 sts on spare needle and complete to match 1st side from ** but work 3 rows straight not 2.

FRONT

Work as back until a total of 3 complete pats have been worked, then work 1st to 12th rows again.

Neck Shaping

1st row (right side) K 36, bind off next 13 sts, K to end.

Cont in st-st on last set of 36 sts for 1st side. Leave rem sts on a spare needle. P 1 row.

*** Bind off 2 sts at beg of next row and on the foll 3 alt rows, then 1 st on the next alt row. 27 sts.

Work 4 rows straight. Bind off loosely.

Next row With wrong side facing, rejoin yarn to inner end of 36 sts on spare needle and complete to match 1st side from *** but work 5 rows straight not 4.

SLEEVES

With No. 10½ needles, cast on 30 sts. Work 2 rows in g-st.

Change to No. 11 needles.

Cont in st-st, inc 1 st at each end of every 3rd row until there are 72 sts.

Cont straight until sleeve measures 16 in (41 cm) from cast-on edge.

Bind off very loosely using a size larger needle.

COLLAR

Joint right shoulder seam.

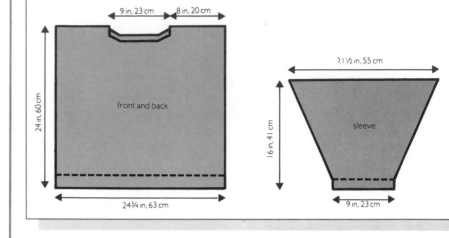

With right side facing and using No. 8 needles, pick up and k 32 sts evenly around front neck and 30 sts around back neck. 62 sts. P 1 row.

Pat row *K 1, k 1 b; rep from * to last 2 sts, k 2.

Rep pat row until collar measures 12½ in (32 cm). Bind off loosely in pat.

FINISHING

Press very lightly.

Join left shoulder and collar seam, reversing collar seam for last 8 in (20 cm) to allow for turn-over. With center of bind-off edge of sleeves to shoulder seams, sew on sleeves. Join side and sleeve seams.

SCARLET

SMOOTH LINES AND CHEVRON STITCHES MAKE THIS THE PERFECT PARTY-GOER, MOVING AND GLITTERING IN THE LIGHT. DESIGNED BY AILEEN SWAN

MATERIALS

21 (23, 25) × 25 g balls Twilleys Goldfingering
No. 1 and No. 2 circular knitting needles, 36 in (100 cm) long
Cable needle
4 circular or extra long needles, No. 2 or less, to be used for shoulder and upper sleeve stitch holders
7 small buttons

MEASUREMENTS

To fit bust 34 (36, 38) in, 86 (91, 97) cm
Acutal measurement – 40½ (42½, 44) in, 103 (108, 112) cm
Length – 24¾ (25¼, 25½) in, 63 (64, 65) cm
Sleeve length – 17¾ in, 45 cm
Figures in parenthesis are for larger sizes

GAUGE

34 sts and 44 rows to 4 in (10 cm) over pat on No. 2 needles

ABBREVIATIONS

alt – alternate; beg – beginning; cm – centimeters; cont – continue; dec – decrease; foll – following; in – inches; inc – increase; k – knit; p – purl; pat pattern; psso – pass slipped stitch over; rem – remain(ing); rep – repeat; rev st-st – reverse stockinette stitch; sl – slip; st(s) – stitch(es); st-st – stockinette stitch

NOTE

Work forwards and back in rows throughout.

BACK

With No. 1 needle, cast on 174 (182, 190) sts.
1st rib row (right side) K 2, *p 2, k 2; rep from * to end.
2nd rib row P 2, *k 2, p 2; rep from * to end.

Rep 1st and 2nd rib rows 3 times, then work 1st rib row again.
Change to No. 2 needle.
Cont from chart thus (noting that chart is in two halves, but should be read as one):
1st row (wrong side) Reading chart from left to right, beg at left-hand line for 1st (2nd, 3rd) size and work 3 (7, 11) sts to dotted line A, work 21 sts between dotted lines A and B 3 times, then work 21 sts between lines B and C once**, now *** work 21 sts

between lines C and D once, then work 21 sts between lines D and E 3 times, work 3 (7, 11) sts beyond line E, thus ending at line for 1st (2nd, 3rd) size.
2nd row Reading chart from right to left, beg at right-hand line for 1st (2nd, 3rd) size and work 3 (7, 11) sts to line E, work 21 sts between lines E and D 3 times, then work 21 sts between lines D and C once**, now *** work 21 sts between lines C and B once, work 21 sts between lines B and A 3 times,

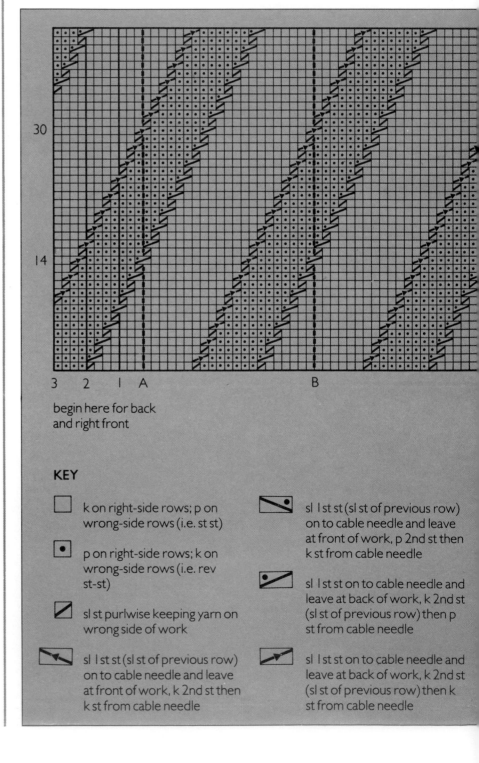

begin here for back and right front

KEY

□	k on right-side rows; p on wrong-side rows (i.e. st st)	⬈•	sl 1st st (sl st of previous row) on to cable needle and leave at front of work, p 2nd st then k st from cable needle
•□	p on right-side rows; k on wrong-side rows (i.e. rev st-st)	•⬈	sl 1st st on to cable needle and leave at back of work, k 2nd st (sl st of previous row) then p st from cable needle
◿	sl st purlwise keeping yarn on wrong side of work		
◺▸	sl 1st st (sl st of previous row) on to cable needle and leave at front of work, k 2nd st then k st from cable needle	◹▸	sl 1st st on to cable needle and leave at back of work, k 2nd st (sl st of previous row) then k st from cable needle

work 3 (7, 11) sts beyond line A, thus ending at line for 1st (2nd, 3rd) size. Cont working each row of chart in this way (see note for 14th and 30th rows) until all 42 rows of chart have been completed. These 42 rows form pat. Beg again at 1st row and cont in pat until the 39th row of the 4th pat from beg has been completed. Work should measure 15¼ in (39 cm) from beg.

Sleeve Shaping
Taking extra sts into pat at each side as

they occur, cast on 5 sts at beg of next 54 rows. 444 (452, 460) sts. Cont in pat until the 9th (13th, 17th) row of the 7th pat from beg has been completed.
Work should measure 24 (24½, 24¾) in, 61 (62, 63) cm from beg.

Neck Shaping
1st row Pat 201 (204, 207) sts, turn. Cont on these sts only for 1st side. Bind off 5 sts at beg of next row and on the foll alt row.

Pat 2 rows. Leave rem 191 (194, 197) sts on a stitch holder.
Next row With right side facing, rejoin yarn to inner end of rem sts, bind off center 42 (44, 46) sts, pat to end. 201 (204, 207) sts.
Bind off 5 sts at beg of next 2 alt rows. Pat 1 row.
Leave rem 191 (194, 197) sts on a stitch holder.

POCKET LININGS
Make 2 With No. 2 needle, cast on 38 sts.
Beg k, work 44 rows in st-st.
Break off yarn and leave sts on a stitch holder.

LEFT FRONT
With No. 1 needle, cast on 87 (91, 95) sts.
1st rib row (right side) *K 2, p 2; rep from * to last 3 sts, k 3.
2nd rib row K 1, p 2, *k 2, p 2; rep from * to end.
Rep 1st and 2nd rib rows 3 times.
Next row Inc in 1st st, rib to end. 88 (92, 96) sts.
Change to No. 2 needle.
Cont from chart thus:
1st row (wrong side) K 1, reading chart from left to right, work as 1st row of back from *** to end.
2nd row Work as 2nd row of back to **, k 1.
Cont in pat in this way, with 1 k st at front edge, until the 11th row of the 2nd pat from beg has been worked.
Pocket Opening row Pat 32 (34, 36) sts, sl next 38 sts on to a stitch holder, pat 38 sts of 1 pocket lining, pat 18 (20, 22) sts.
Cont in pat until the 35th row of the 3rd pat from beg has been worked.

Front Shaping
1st row Pat to last 3 sts, k 2 tog, k 1. Keeping pat correct, cont to dec 1 st in this way at end of every foll 4th row until the 39th row of the 4th pat from beg has been worked. 76 (80, 84) sts.

Sleeve Shaping
Cont to dec at front edge as set, AND AT THE SAME TIME, cast on 5 sts at beg of next row and on the foll 26 alt rows, taking sts into pat as they occur. 198 (202, 206) sts.
Now dec at neck edge on 6th row from last dec and every foll 6th row until 191 (194, 197) sts rem.

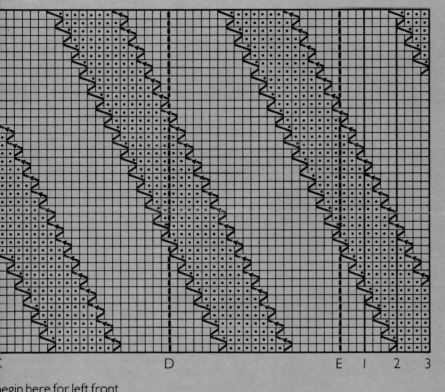

C   D   E   1   2   3

Begin here for left front

NOTE
On 14th and 30th rows of chart dotted lines cut through twist st symbols but this does not change the method of working the twists.
Reading from the right, at dotted line E the 1st half of the twist is shown before the line and the 2nd half after; in the same way in the repeated section between dotted lines E and D, the 1st half of the twist is shown before dotted line D and the 2nd half on the next repeat after dotted line E. Similarly, at the left-hand side of the chart the 1st

half of the twist is before dotted line B and the 2nd half after; in the repeated section between dotted lines B and A, the 1st half of the twist is shown before dotted line A and the 2nd half on the next repeat after dotted line B.

Work left back and left front seam in the same way.

FRONT BAND

With right side facing and using No. I needle, pick up and k 104 sts evenly up straight edge of right front, 140 (144, 148) sts up shaped edge to shoulder, 66 (66, 70) sts around back neck, 140 (144, 148) sts down shaped edge of left front and 104 sts down straight edge of left front. 554 (562, 574) sts.

Beg with 1st rib row of back, rib 3 rows.

Buttonhole row P 2, k 2, bind off 2 sts, *rib 14 including st rem on needle after binding off, bind off 2 sts; rep from * 5 times, rib to end.

Next row Rib to end, casting on 2 sts over each bind-off group. Rib 3 rows. Bind off evenly in rib.

CUFFS

With right side facing and using No. I needle, pick up and k 78 (82, 86) sts evenly across straight edge of sleeve.

Dec row P 0 (0, 2), k 0 (2, 2), p 1, p 2 tog, *k 2, p 1, p 2 tog; rep from * 14 times, k 0 (2, 2), p 0 (0, 2). 62 (66, 70) sts.

Beg with 1st (2nd, 1st) rib row of back, work in rib for 2 in (5 cm). Bind off loosely.

POCKET TOPS

With right side facing, sl sts of pocket onto No. I needle.

Beg with 1st rib row of back, rib 7 rows. Bind off loosely in rib.

FINISHING

Press lightly. Join side and sleeve seams. Sew on buttons. Sew down pocket linings and sides of pocket tops.

Pat straight until the 15th (19th, 23rd) row of the 7th pat from beg has been worked. Leave sts on a stitch holder.

RIGHT FRONT

With No. I needle, cast on 87 (91, 95) sts.

1st row rib (right side) K 3, *p 2, k 2; rep from * to end.

2nd rib row *P 2, k 2; rep from * to last 3 sts, p 2, k 1.

Rep 1st and 2nd rib rows 3 times.

Next row Rib to last st, inc in last st. 88 (92, 96) sts.

Change to No. 2 needle.

Cont from chart thus:

1st row (wrong side) Work as 1st row of back to **, k 1.

2nd row K 1, reading chart from right to left, work as 2nd row of back from *** to end.

Cont in pat as set and complete to match left front, reversing pocket opening row by reading from end to beg; reversing front shapings by working dec as sl 1, k 1, psso at beg instead of end of rows and reversing

sleeve shaping by working 1 row more before sleeve shaping.

SHOULDER SEAMS

With right sides of right back and right front tog and stitch holder needles parallel, with No. 2 needle, beg at end of sleeve and k 1 st from each needle tod, AND AT THE SAME TIME, bind off to end.

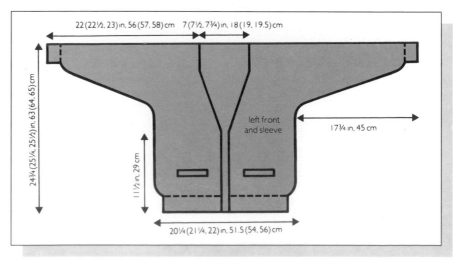

22 (22½, 23) in, 56 (57, 58) cm   7 (7½, 7¾) in, 18 (19, 19.5) cm

24¾ (25¼, 25½) in, 63 (64, 65) cm

11½ in, 29 cm

left front and sleeve

17¾ in, 45 cm

20¼ (21¼, 22) in, 51.5 (54, 56) cm

CAFE SOCIETY

VERMILION

A PLUNGING SHAWL COLLAR MAKES IMMEDIATE IMPACT, WHILE CABLED RIBS AND AN EMBOSSED STITCH ARE THE MORE SUBTLE DETAILS OF THIS SMOULDERING SWEATER. DESIGNED BY BETTY BARNDEN

MATERIALS
14 (15) × 25 g balls 3 Suisses Soiree
Pair each No. 0 and No. 3 knitting needles
No. 1 and No. 0 circular knitting needles, 36 in (100 cm) long
Cable needle

MEASUREMENTS
To fit bust 32-34 (36-38) in, 81-86 (91-97) cm
Actual measurement – 38 (43) in, 96 (110) cm
Length – 26¾ (27½) in, 68 (70) cm
Sleeve length – 17 (17¾) in, 43 (45) cm
Figures in parenthesis are for larger size

GAUGE
35 sts and 42 rows to 4 in (10 cm) measured over pat of chart on No. 3 needles

ABBREVIATIONS
alt – alternate; beg – beginning; c 4 b – sl next 2 sts on to cable needle and hold at back, k 2 then k 2 from cable needle; cm – centimeters; cont – continue; dec – decrease; foll – following; in – inches; inc – increase; k – knit; p – purl; pat – pattern; psso – pass slipped stitch over; rem – remain(ing); rep – repeat; sl – slip; st(s) – stitch(es); tbl – through back of loops; tog – together

BACK
With No. 0 needles, cast on 164 (184) sts.
Work in cable rib pat thus:
1st row (right side) K 1, *k 2, p 2, k 4, p 2; rep from * to last 3 sts, k 3.
2nd row K 1, *p 2, k 2, p 4, k 2; rep from * to last 3 sts, p 2, k 1.

3rd row K 1, *k 2, p 2, c 4 b, p 2; rep from * to last 3 sts, k 3.
4th row As 2nd.
These 4 rows form cable rib pat.
Rep 1st to 4th rows 6 times, then work 1st to 3rd rows again.
Inc row Pat 14 (11), *inc in next st, pat 26 (17); rep from * 4 (8) times, inc in next st, pat 14 (10). 170 (194) sts.
Change to No. 3 needles.
Cont in pat from chart thus:
1st row (right side) K 1, reading row 1 of chart from right to left, rep the 24 sts to last st, k 1.
2nd row K 1, reading row 2 of chart from left to right, rep the 24 sts to last st, k 1.
Beg with row 3 of chart, cont until row 32 has been worked **.
Rep the 32 rows of chart 3 times, then work rows 1 to 18 (1 to 20) again.
A total of 146 (148) rows of pat have been worked from top of rib.
Mark each end of last row with a thread to denote start of armholes.
Work rows 19 to 32 (21 to 32).
Rep the 32 rows of chart 2 (3) times.
1st size only: Work rows 1 to 24.
Both sizes: 102 (108) rows have been worked after markers.

Neck Shaping
1st row (right side) Pat 43 (55) sts, turn.
Keeping pat correct, cont on these sts only for 1st side. Leave rem sts on a

spare needle.
2nd row P 2 tog, pat to end.
3rd row Pat to last 2 sts, k 2 tog.
Rep 2nd and 3rd rows twice, 37 (49) sts.
Pat 1 row, thus ending with row 32 (8).

Shoulder Shaping
Bind off 9 (12) sts at beg of next row and on the foll 2 alt rows. Pat 1 row.
Bind off rem 10 (13) sts.
Next row With right side facing, sl center 84 sts on to a spare needle, rejoin yarn to inner end of rem 43 (55) sts and pat to end.
Next row Pat to last 2 sts, p 2 tog tbl.
Next row Sl 1, k 1, psso, pat to end.
Rep last 2 rows twice, 37 (49) sts. Pat 2 rows, thus ending with row 1 (9).

Shoulder Shaping
Work as for 1st side.

FRONT
Work as back to **.
Rep 32 rows of chart once.

Neck Shaping
1st row (right side) Pat 85 (97) sts, turn.
Keeping pat correct, cont on these sts only for 1st side.
Leave rem sts on a spare needle.
2nd row Pat to end.
3rd row Pat to last 2 sts, k 2 tog.

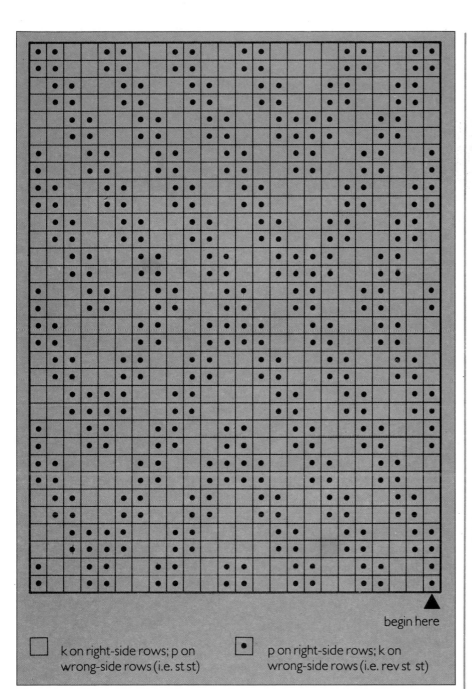

□	k on right-side rows; p on wrong-side rows (i.e. st st)
▣	p on right-side rows; k on wrong-side rows (i.e. rev st st)

begin here

4th row until there are 128 (132) sts, working inc sts into pat.

Inc 1 st at each end of every right-side row until there are 182 (194) sts.

Pat straight until sleeve measures 18½ (19¼) in, 47 (49) cm from cast-on edge, ending with a wrong-side row. Bind off.

NECKBAND
Join shoulder seams.

With right side facing and using No. 1 circular needle, pick up and k 163 (168) sts evenly up right front neck and 12 sts down right back neck, k across 84 sts at center back, pick up and k 12 sts up left back neck and 163 (168) sts down left front neck. 434 (444) sts. Work forwards and back in rows. Beg with 2nd row, work 27 rows in cable rib pat, ending with a 4th row. Change to No. 0 circular needle and pat a further 28 rows. Bind off in rib.

MAKING UP
Sew on sleeves between markers. Join side and sleeve seams, reversing seam for turn-back cuff. Overlap neckband at center front as shown and sew row-ends to sides of neck shaping.

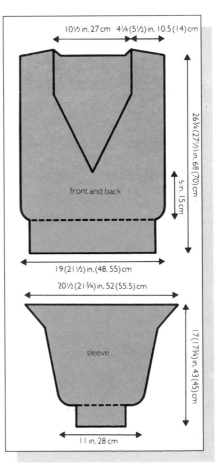

Rep last 2 rows until 61 (73) sts rem, ending with a wrong-side row.

Dec 1 st at neck edge on next row and every foll 4th row until 53 (64) sts rem, ending with a right-side row. Pat 3 (1) rows.

Mark armhole edge of last row with a contrast thread.

Cont to dec on every 4th row from previous dec until 37 (49) sts rem.

Pat straight until front matches back to shoulder, ending at side edge.

Shoulder Shaping
Work as for back.

Next row With right side facing, rejoin yarn to inner end of 85 (97) sts on spare needle and pat to end.

Next row Pat to end.

Next row Sl 1, k 1, psso, pat to end. Complete to match 1st side.

SLEEVES
With No. 0 needles, cast on 84 sts.

Work 32 rows in cable rib pat as back.

Inc row Pat 3, *inc in next st, pat 5; rep from * 12 times, inc in next st, pat 2. 98 sts.

Change to No. 3 needles.

NOTE
Wrong side of cuff is facing as row 1 of chart is worked to allow for turn back.

Cont from chart as given for back, inc 1 st at each end of 5th row and every foll

DEEP PURPLE

A SKIMPY LITTLE SINGLET AND A LUXURIOUS SMOKING JACKET BRING THE TWINSET INTO THE EXCITING EIGHTIES. DESIGNED BY BETTY BARNDEN

MATERIALS

Jacket
16 (17, 17, 18) × 25 g balls Avocet Alpaca Mohair shade 105 (M)
3 × 50 g balls Avocet Soiree shade 511 (A)
Pair each No. 6 and No. 8 knitting needles
No. 8 circular needle 36 in (100 cm) long
Shoulder pads

Singlet
7 (8, 9, 9) × 50 g balls Avocet Soiree shade 511
Pair each No. 6 and No. 8 knitting needles

MEASUREMENTS

Jacket
To fit bust 32 (34, 36, 38) in, 81 (86, 91, 97) cm
Actual measurement – 41 (43, 45, 47) in, 104 (109, 114, 120) cm
Length – 24½ (25¼, 26, 26¾) in, 62 (64, 66, 68) cm
Sleeve length – 17 in, 43 cm

Singlet
To fit bust 32 (34, 36, 38) in, 81 (86, 91, 97) cm
Actual measurement – 31½ (33½, 35½, 37½) in, 80 (85, 90, 95) cm
Length – 22 (22½, 23, 23¼) in, 56 (57, 58, 59) cm
Figures in parenthesis are for larger sizes

GAUGE

Jacket
15 st and 20 rows to 4 in (10 cm) measured over st-st on No. 8 needles using M.

Singlet
24 sts and 30 rows to 4 in (10 cm) measured over diagonal rib on No. 8 needles

ABBREVIATIONS

alt – alternate; beg – beginning; cm – centimeters; cont – continue; dec – decrease; foll – following; in – inches; inc – increase; k – knit; m 1 – make 1 st by picking up the strand between sts and k it through the back of the loop; p – purl; pat – pattern; rem – remain(ing); rep – repeat; sl – slip; st(s) – stitch(es); st-st – stockinette stitch; tog – together

DEEP PURPLE

JACKET
BACK
With No. 6 needles and A, cast on 80 (84, 88, 92) sts. Work 12 rows st-st. Change to No. 8 needles and M. Fold work in half with cast-on edge behind sts on needle.

Next row (close hem) *K next st from needle tog with corresponding st from cast-on edge; rep from * to end. **
Beg with a p row, work in st-st.
Cont straight until back measures 15¾ (16, 16½, 17) in, 40 (41, 42, 43) cm, ending with a p row.

Armhole Shaping
Bind off 6 sts at beg of next 2 rows. Dec 1 st at each end of every right-side row until 56 (60, 64, 68) sts rem. Cont straight until work measures 24½ (25¼, 26, 26¾) in, 62 (64, 66, 68) cm, ending with a p row.

Shoulder Shaping
Bind off 6 (6, 6, 7) sts at beg of next 4 rows, then bind off 5 (6, 7, 6) sts at beg of next 2 rows.
Bind off rem 22 (24, 26, 28) sts.

POCKET LININGS
Make 2 With No. 8 needles and M, cast on 26 sts.
Work in st-st for 28 rows. Break yarn and leave sts on a stitch holder.

LEFT FRONT
With No. 6 needles and A, cast on 40 (42, 44, 46) sts. Work as back to **
Beg with a p row, work 29 rows st-st.
***

Pocket Opening row K 8 (10, 12, 14) sts, sl next 26 sts on to a stitch holder, k across sts of one pocket lining, k 6. P 1 row.

Front Shaping
1st row K to last st, m 1, k 1.
Cont to inc at front edge thus on every foll 6th row until front matches back to armhole, ending with a p row.

Armhole Shaping
Bind off 6 sts at beg of next row, then dec 1 st at armhole edge on next 6 right-side rows, AT THE SAME TIME inc at front edge as before.
Keeping armhole edge straight, cont to inc at front edge until there are 43 (45, 47, 49) sts.
Work straight until front matches back to shoulder, ending with a p row.

Shoulder Shaping
Bind off 6 (6, 6, 7) sts at beg of next row and on the foll alt row.
P 1 row. Bind off 5 (6, 7, 6) sts at beg of next row.
Work 13 (15, 17, 19) rows straight on rem 26 (27, 28, 29) sts. Bind off.

RIGHT FRONT
Work as left front to ***.
Pocket Opening row K 6, sl next 26 sts on to a stitch holder, k across sts of 2nd pocket lining, k 8 (10, 12, 14). P 1 row.

Front Shaping
1st row K 1, m 1, k to end.

Complete to match left front, working 1 extra row before armhole shaping and shoulder shaping.

SLEEVES
With No. 6 needles and A, cast on 50 (52, 54, 56) sts.
Work as back to **.
Beg with a p row, work in st-st.
Inc 1 st at each end of every 10th (10th, 8th, 8th) row until there are 64 (68, 72, 76) sts.
Cont straight until sleeve measures 17 in (43 cm), ending with a p row.

Cap Shaping
Bind off 6 sts at beg of next 2 rows.
Dec 1 st at each end of every right-side row until 32 (36, 40, 44) sts rem, ending with a p row.
Dec 1 st at each end of every row until 24 sts rem. Bind off.

POCKET TOPS
With right side facing, using No. 6 needles and A, k across 26 sts on stitch holder. Beg p, work 11 rows st-st. Bind off.

RIGHT FRONT BAND
With right side facing, using No. 6 circular needle and A, pick up and k 4 sts from edge of lower hem, pick up and k evenly 139 (144, 148, 153) sts along rem front edge and collar extension. 143 (148, 152, 157) sts.
Beg p, work 11 rows st-st. Bind off or leave sts on spare yarn (see finishing).

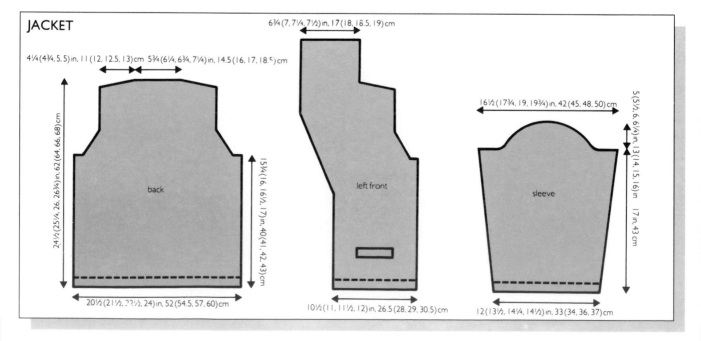

JACKET

6¾ (7, 7¼, 7½) in, 17 (18, 18.5, 19) cm

4¼ (4¾, 5, 5) in, 11 (12, 12.5, 13) cm   5¾ (6¼, 6¾, 7¼) in, 14.5 (16, 17, 18.5) cm

24½ (25¼, 26, 26¾) in, 62 (64, 66, 68) cm

15¾ (16, 16½, 17) in, 40 (41, 42, 43) cm

16½ (17¾, 19, 19¾) in, 42 (45, 48, 50) cm

5 (5½, 6, 6¼) in, 13 (14, 15, 16) in   17 in, 43 cm

back

left front

sleeve

20½ (21½, 22½, 24) in, 52 (54.5, 57, 60) cm

10½ (11, 11½, 12) in, 26.5 (28, 29, 30.5) cm

12 (13½, 14¼, 14½) in, 33 (34, 36, 37) cm

LEFT FRONT BAND
Work to match right front band.

FINISHING
Press lightly, omitting edgings. Join shoulder seams. Join bind-off edges of collar extensions and row ends of bands with seam to inside of folded collar. Centering this seam at back neck, sew down collar. Fold and hem front band, either whipstitching carefully a bind-off edge (remembering that this will be the right side on collar), or grafting sts left on spare yarn taking care to match each st loop with a picked-up st. Hem pocket tops. Set in sleeves. Join side and sleeve seams.

SINGLET
BACK
With No. 6 needles, cast on 98 (104, 110, 116) sts.
1st rib row (right side) K 1, *p 3, k 3; rep from * to last st, k 1.
2nd row P 1, * p 3, k 3; rep from * to last st, p 1.
Rep these 2 rows 7 times.
Change to No. 8 needles.
Cont in pat thus:
1st row (right side) K 4, *p 3, k 3; rep from * to last 4 sts, p 3, k 1.
2nd row P 1, *k 3, p 3; rep from * to last st, p 1.
3rd row *K 3, p 3; rep from * to last 2 sts, k 2.
4th row P 2, *k 3, p 3; rep from * to end.
5th row K 2, *p 3, k 3; rep from * to end.
6th row *P 3, k 3; rep from * to last 2 sts, p 2.
7th row K 1, *p 3, k 3; rep from * to last st, k 1.
8th row P 4, *k 3, p 3; rep from * to last 4 sts, k 3, p 1.
9th row K 1, p 2, *k 3, p 3; rep from * to last 5 sts, k 3, p 1, k 1.
10th row P 1, k 1, *p 3, k 3; rep from * to last 6 sts, p 3, k 2, p 1.
11th row K 1, p 1, *k 3, p 3; rep from * to last 6 sts, k 3, p 2, k 1.
12th row P 1, k 2, *p 3, k 3; rep from * to last 5 sts, p 3, k 1, p 1.
These 12 rows form pat.
Rep pat 7 times, 96 rows.

Armhole Shaping
Keeping pat correct, bind off 12 sts at beg of next 2 rows.
Dec 1 st at each end of next 12 (14, 14, 16) rows, then on the foll 3 (4, 4, 5) alt rows. 44 (44, 50, 50) sts. **
Pat 12 rows without shaping.

Neck Shaping
1st row Pat 16 sts, turn.
Cont on these sts only for 1st side and leave rem sts on a spare needle.
Bind off 3 sts at beg of next row.
Dec 1 st at neck edge on next 5 rows, then on the foll 2 alt rows. 6 sts.
Pat straight for 16 (14, 16, 14) rows.
Bind off.
Next row With right side facing, sl center 12 (12, 18, 18) sts on to stitch holder, rejoin yarn to inner end of rem 16 sts and pat to end.
Complete to match 1st side.

FRONT
Work as back to **.
Complete as back from neck shaping but pat 12 extra rows straight before binding off.

NECK EDGING
Join left shoulder strap.
With right side facing and using No. 6 needles, pick up and k22 sts. evenly down right back neck, k 12 (12, 18, 18) sts across center back, pick up and k 22 sts up left back neck, pick up and k 30 sts down left front neck, k 12 (12, 18, 18) sts across center, pick up and k 30 sts up right front neck. 128 (128, 140, 140) sts. K 1 row. Bind off.

ARMHOLE EDGINGS
Join right shoulder strap.
With right side facing and using No. 6 needles, pick up and k 116 (120, 124, 130) sts evenly around armhole. K 1 row. Bind off.

FINISHING
Join side seams.

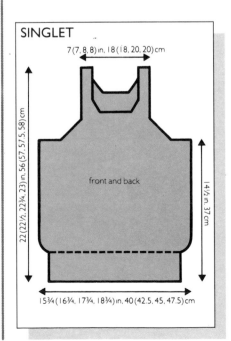

SINGLET

7 (7, 8, 8) in, 18 (18, 20, 20) cm

22 (22½, 22¾, 23) in, 56 (57, 57.5, 58) cm

front and back

14½ in, 37 cm

15¾ (16¾, 17¾, 18¾) in, 40 (42.5, 45, 47.5) cm

INDIAN SUMMER

INDIAN SUMMER

DELHI

AN ESSENTIALLY FEMININE CRICKET SWEATER COMBINES A SOPHISTICATED YARN AND SOFTLY WRAPPED CABLES. DESIGNED BY PAT QUIROGA

MATERIALS
8 (9, 10) × 50 g balls Tootal Avalon
Pair each No. 6 and No. 8 knitting
needles
Cable needle
Shoulder pads

MEASUREMENTS
To fit bust 34 (36, 38) in, 86 (91, 97) cm
Actual measurement – 42½ (44½,
46½) in, 108 (113, 118) cm
Length – 27½ in, 70 cm
Sleeve length – 17¼ in, 44 cm
Figures in parenthesis are for larger
sizes

GAUGE
16 st and 20 rows to 4 in (10 cm) over
st-st on No. 8 needles

ABBREVIATIONS
beg – beginning; c 15 b – sl next 7 sts
on to cable needle and leave at back of
work, k 8 then k 7 from cable needle;
c 15 f – sl next 8 sts on to cable needle
and leave at front of work, k 7 then k 8
from cable needle; cm – centimeters;
cont – continue; dec – decrease; foll –
following; in – inches; inc – increase;
k – knit; m 1 – make 1 st by picking up
the strand between sts and k it through
the back of the loop; p – purl; pat –
pattern; psso – pass slipped stitch over;
rem – remain(ing); rep – repeat; sl –
slip; st(s) – stitch(es); st-st – stockinette

D·E·L·H·I

stitch; tog – together; wyib – with yarn in back of work; wyif – with yarn in front of work
Work instructions in square brackets the number of times given

BACK

With No. 6 needles, cast on 76 (76, 84) sts.
1st rib row (right side) K 1, *k 2, p 2; rep from * to last 3 sts, k 3.
2nd rib row K 1, *p 2, k 2; rep from * to last 3 sts, p 2, k 1.
Rep 1st and 2nd rib rows 16 times, then work 1st rib row again.
Next row Rib 2, [m 1, rib 4] 5 (7, 5) times, m 1, rib 32 (16, 40), [m 1, rib 4] 5 (7, 5) times m 1, rib 2.
88 (92, 96) sts.
Change to No. 8 needles.

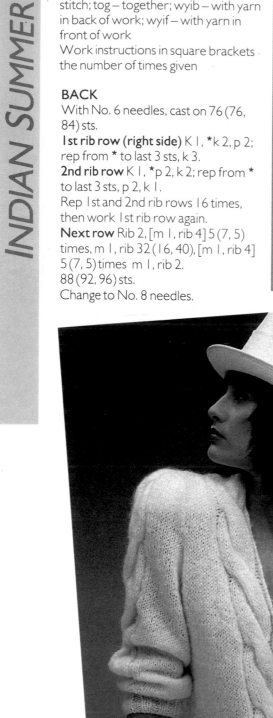

Cont in st-st. Work 76 (74, 72) rows.

Armhole Shaping
Bind off 6 (7, 8) sts at beg of next 2 rows.
Dec 1 st at each end of the next 8 rows. 60 (62, 64) sts.
Work 22 (24, 26) rows straight.

Neck Shaping
1st row K 11 (12, 13), bind off next 38 sts, k to end.
Cont on last 11 (12, 13) sts only for 1st side.
Dec 1 st at neck edge on the next 5 rows.
Bind off rem 6 (7, 8) sts.
With wrong side facing, rejoin yarn to inner end of rem 11 (12, 13) sts and

complete to match 1st side.

FRONT

With No. 6 needles, cast on 86 (86, 94) sts.
1st row (right side) K 1, [k 2, p 2] 6 (6, 7) times, *k 4, [wyif, sl 1, wyib, k 1] 3 times, wyif, sl 1, wyib, k 4*, p 2, k 2, p 2 **k 4, [sl 1, k 1] 3 times, sl 1, k 4**, [p 2, k 2] 6 (6, 7) times, k 1.
2nd row K 1, [p 2, k 2] 6 (6, 7) times, **p 5, [wyib, sl 1, wyif, p 1] 3 times, p 4**, k 2, p 2, k 2, *p 5, [sl 1, p 1] 3 times, p 4*, [k 2, p 2] 6 (6, 7) times, k 1.
3rd row Rib 25 (25, 29), *k 4 [sl next st on to cable needle and leave at back of work, k 1] 3 times, k the 3 sts from cable needle, k 5*, p 2, k 2, p 2, **k 4, [sl next st on to cable needle and leave at front of work, k 1] 3 times, k 3 from cable needle, k 5**, rib 25 (25, 29).
4th row Rib 25 (25, 29), p 15, k 2, p 2, k 2, p 15, rib 25 (25, 29).
Now beg cable pat over center 40 sts thus:
1st row Rib 23 (23, 27), p 2, k 15, p 2, k 2, p 2, k 15, p 2, rib 23 (23, 27).
2nd row Rib 23 (23, 27), k 2, p 15, k 2, p 2, k 2, p 15, k 2, rib 23 (23, 27).
3rd to 12 rows Rep 1st and 2nd rows 5 times.
13th row Rib 23 (23, 27), p 2, c 15 b, p 2, k 2, p 2, c 15 f, p 2, rib 23 (23, 27).
14th row As 2nd.
15th to 20th rows Work 1st and 2nd rows 3 times.
These 20 rows set cable pat over center 40 sts.
Rep 1st to 11th rows.
Next row [Rib 2, m 1] 7 (11, 5) times, [rib 4, m 1] 2 (0, 4) times, p 1, work 12th row of cable pat over next 40 sts, p 1, [m 1, rib 4] 2 (0, 4) times, [m 1, rib 2] 7 (11, 5) times.
104 (108, 112) sts.
Change to No. 8 needles.
Cont in cable pat over center 40 sts but change to st-st over 32 (34, 36) sts at each side.
Work 66 (64, 62) rows.

Neck Shaping
1st row K 30 (32, 34), k 2 tog, pat 20 sts, turn.
Cont on these sts only for 1st side.
Keeping pat correct, pat 3 rows.
Dec row K to last 22 sts, k 2 tog, pat 20.
Pat 3 rows.
Rep dec row.
Pat 1 row, 49 (51, 53) sts.

***Armhole Shaping

Cont to dec at neck on every 4th row from previous dec as before, AND AT THE SAME TIME, bind of 6 (7, 8) sts at beg of next row.

Pat I row – omit this row on 2nd side.

Dec I st at armhole edge on the next 8 rows.

Cont to dec at neck only until 26 (27, 28) sts rem ***

Pat 3 (5, 7) rows straight, thus ending at armhole edge.

Shoulder Shaping

Next row Bind off 5 (6, 7) sts, pat to end. 21 sts.

Next row K 3, p 7, wyib, sl I, wyif, turn.

Next row Sl I, k 7, p 2, k I.

Next row K 3, p 15, k 3.

Back Extension

Ist row (right side) K I, p 2, k 15, p 2, k I.

2nd row K 3, p 15, k 3.

3rd row K I, p 2, k 9, wyif, sl I, wyib, turn.

4th row Sl I, p 9, k 3.

5th row K I, p 2, k 4, wyif, sl I, wyib, turn.

6th row Sl I, p 4, k 3.

7th to 14th rows Rep Ist to 6th rows once, then work Ist and 2nd rows again.

15th row K I, p 2, c 15 b, p 2, k I.

16th row As 2nd.

17th to 30th rows Rep Ist to 6th rows twice, then work Ist and 2nd rows again.

Bind off. Mark last bind-off st with a colored thread.

With right side facing rejoin yarn to inner end of rem 52 (54, 56) sts.

Dec row Pat 20, sl I, k I, psso, k to end.

Pat 3 rows.

Rep last 4 rows once.

Rep dec row. Pat 2 rows. 49 (51, 53) sts. Work to match Ist side from *** to ***.

Pat 4 (6, 8) rows straight, thus ending at armhole edge.

Shoulder Shaping

Next row Bind off 5 (6, 7) sts, pat to end. 21 sts.

Next row K I, p 2, k 7, wyib, sl I, wyib, turn.

Next row Sl I, p 7, k 3.

Back Extension

Ist row K I, p 2, k 15, p 2, k I.

2nd row K 3, p 9, wyib, sl I, wyif, turn.

3rd row Sl I, k 9, p 2, k I.

4th row K 3, p 4, wyib, sl I, wyif, turn.

5th row Sl I, k 4, p 2, k I.

6th row K 3, p 15, k 3.

7th to 12th rows As Ist to 6th rows.

13th row As Ist.

14th row As 6th.

15th row K I, p 2, c 15 f, p 2, k I.

16th row As 6th.

17th to 28th rows Rep Ist to 6th rows twice.

29th row As Ist.

30th row As 6th.

Bind off.

RIGHT SLEEVE

With No. 6 needles, cast on 41 sts.

Ist row (right side) K I, [k 2, p 2] 3 times, work from * to * of Ist row of front rib, [p 2, k 2] 2 times, k I.

2nd row K I, [p 2, k 2] 3 times, work from * to * of 2nd row of front rib [k 2, p 2] 3 times, k I.

3rd row Rib 13, work from * to * of 3rd row of front rib, rib 13.

4th row Rib 13, p 15, rib 13.

Now beg cable pat over center 19 sts thus:

Ist row Rib 11, p 2, k 15, p 2, rib 11.

2nd row Rib 11, k 2, p 15, k 2, rib 11.

3rd to 12th rows Rep Ist and 2nd rows 5 times.

13th row Rib 11, p 2, c 15 b, p 2, rib 11.

14th row As 2nd.

15th row As Ist.

16th row [Rib 2, m I] 5 times, p 1, k 2, p 15, k 2, p I, [m I, rib 2] 5 times. 51 sts.

Change to No. 8 needles.

17th row K 16, p 2, k 15, p 2, k 16.

18th row P 16, k 2, p 15, k 2, p 16.

19th and 20th rows As 17th and 18th rows.

These 20 rows set cable pat over center 19 sts.

Cont in cable pat over center 19 sts working in st-st over rem sts.

Inc I st at each end of next row and every foll 4th row until there are 71 (73, 75) sts.

Pat 31 (27, 23) rows straight.

Cap Shaping

Keeping pat correct, bind off 6 (7, 8) sts at beg of next 2 rows.

Dec I st at each end of next 8 rows. 43 sts.

Work 20 (22, 24) rows straight.

Next row [K 3 tog] 4 times, p 2 tog, [k 3 tog] 3 times, [sl I, k 2 tog, psso] twice,

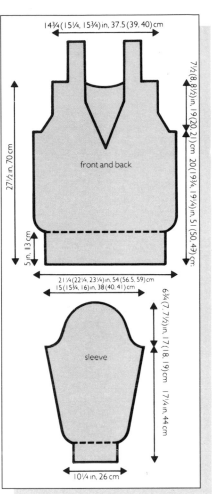

p 2 tog, [sl I, k 2 tog, psso] 4 times. 15 sts.

Next row P.

Next row [K 2 tog] 3 times, k 3, [sl I, k I, psso] 3 times.

Next row P.

Bind off rem 9 sts.

LEFT SLEEVE

Work as right sleeve but on Ist to 3rd rows of cuff work from ** to ** of front rib not from * to *. Work c 15 f instead of c 15 b.

NECK EDGING

With right side facing, using No. 6 needles and beg at marker on left back extension, pick up and k 60 (62, 64) sts evenly to center of 'V' and 60 (62, 64) sts evenly to bind-off edge of right back extension. Bind off knitwise.

FINISHING

Join shoulder seams. Join bind-off edges of back extensions, then with seam to center back neck, sew in place. Join side and sleeve seams. Set in sleeves. Sew in shoulder pads. Press seams.

MADRAS

A TOWELLING-TEXTURED SPORTS SHIRT HAS PADDED SHOULDERS AND A DEEP CABLED RIB. DESIGNED BY LESLEY STANFIELD

MATERIALS

11 (12, 12, 13) 50 g balls Copley Sandpiper
Pair each No. 3 and No. 4 knitting needles
Set of four No. 3 double-pointed needles
Cable needle
Shoulder pads

MEASUREMENTS

To fit bust 32 (34, 36, 38) in, 81 (86, 91, 97) cm
Actual measurement – 38 (40, 42½, 45) in, 96 (102, 108, 114) cm
Length – 25¼, (25½, 26, 26½) in, 64 (65, 66, 67) cm
Sleeve length – 17 in, 43 cm
Figures in parenthesis are for larger sizes

GAUGE

20 sts and 28 rows to 4 in (10 cm) over st-st on No. 4 needles

ABBREVIATIONS

alt – alternate; beg – beginning; c 4 – sl next 2 sts on to cable needle and hold at front, k 2 then k 2 from cable needle; cm – centimeters; cont – continue; dec – decrease; foll – following; g-st – garter st; in – inches; inc – increase; k – knit; m 1 – make 1 st by picking up the strand between sts and k it through the back of the loop; p – purl; rem – remain(ing); rep – repeat; sl – slip: st(s) – stitch(es); st-st – stockinette stitch; tog – together
Work instructions in square brackets the number of times given

BACK

With pair of No. 3 needles, cast on 77 (82, 87, 92) sts.
1st row (right side) P 2, *k 3, p 2; rep from * to end.
2nd row K 2, *p 3, k 2; rep from * to end.

3rd row As 1st.

4th row K 2, *p twice into next st, p 2, k 2; rep from * to end. 92 (98, 104, 110) sts.

5th row P 2, *c 4, p 2; rep from * to end.

6th row K 2, *p 4, k 2; rep from * to end.

7th row P 2, *k 4, p 2; rep from * to end. .

8th row As 6th.

9th row As 7th.

10th row As 6th.

Rep 5th to 10th rows 4 times, then work 5th to 7th rows again.

Change to No. 4 needles.

Next row (wrong side) P.

Cont in st-st, inc 1 st at each end of every 20th row until there are 98 (104, 110, 116) sts.

Cont straight until work measures 15¾ in (40 cm) ending with a wrong-side row.

Armhole shaping

Dec 1 st at each end of every row until 70 (76, 82, 88) sts rem. *

Cont straight until work measures 25¼ (25½, 26, 26½) in, 64 (65, 66, 67) cm ending with a wrong-side row.

Leave sts on a spare needle.

FRONT

Work as back to *.

Cont straight until work measures 23 (23¼, 24, 24) in, 58 (59, 60, 61) cm ending with a wrong-side row.

Neck Shaping

1st row K 31 (33, 35, 37) sts, turn.

Cont on these sts only for 1st side.

Leave rem sts on a spare needle.

Dec 1 st at neck edge on the next 8 rows. 23 (25, 27, 29) sts.

Cont straight until front matches back to shoulder. Leave sts on a holder.

Next row With right side facing, sl center 8 (10, 12, 14) sts on to a stitch holder, rejoin yarn to inner end of rem 31 (33, 35, 37) sts and k to end.

Complete to match 1st side.

SLEEVES

With pair of No. 3 needles, cast on 38 (42, 46, 50) sts.

Work 6 rows g-st.

Change to No. 4 needles.

Cont in st-st, inc 1 st at each end of 1st and every foll 4th row until there are 90 (94, 98, 102) sts, ending with a wrong-side row.

Inc 1 st at each end of next and alt rows until there are 104 (108, 112, 116) sts, ending with a wrong-side row.

Cap Shaping

Dec 1 st at each end of every row until 76 (80, 84, 88) sts rem. Bind off loosely.

COLLAR

Join right shoulder seam thus: place wrong sides tog. With back facing and using No. 4 needles, bind off first 23 (25, 27, 29) sts from back and all right front shoulder sts tog knitwise, taking 1 st from each needle tog each time. Sl 24 (26, 28, 30) sts from center back on to a stitch holder. Join left shoulder as for right shoulder.

Mark center of front neck with a contrast thread.

With right side facing and No. 3 double pointed needles, k 4 (5, 6, 7) sts from side of center front marker, pick up and k evenly 16 sts up right front neck, k across 24 (26, 28, 30) sts of back neck, pick up and k 16 sts down left front neck, k 4 (5, 6, 7) sts from other side of center front marker. 64 (68, 72, 76) sts.

Working forwards and back in rows, work 8 rows g-st.

Next row K 4 (5, 6, 7), [m 1, k 3] 4 times, [m 1, k 2] 4 times, m 1, k 16 (18, 20, 22), [m 1, k 2] 4 times, [m 1, k 3] 4 times, m 1, k 4 (5, 6, 7). 82 (86, 90, 94) sts.

Work 14 rows g-st. Bind off loosely.

FINISHING

Press, omitting cables and g-st. Set in sleeves. Join side and sleeve seams. Sew in shoulder pads.

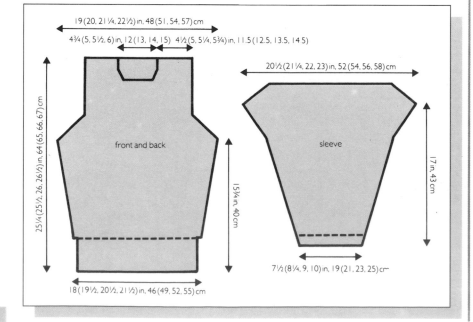

19 (20, 21¼, 22½) in, 48 (51, 54, 57) cm

4¾ (5, 5½, 6) in, 12 (13, 14, 15)   4½ (5, 5¼, 5¾) in, 11.5 (12.5, 13.5, 14.5)

20½ (21¼, 22, 23) in, 52 (54, 56, 58) cm

front and back

sleeve

25¼ (25½, 26, 26½) in, 64 (65, 66, 67) cm

15¾ in, 40 cm

17 in, 43 cm

18 (19½, 20½, 21½) in, 46 (49, 52, 55) cm

7½ (8¼, 9, 10) in, 19 (21, 23, 25) cm

JAIPUR

A WIDE, WIDE T-SHIRT IN CHALKY COTTON IS PUNCTUATED BY CLUSTERS OF SMALL CABLES. DESIGNED BY DEBBIE BLISS

MATERIALS
16 × 50 g balls Hayfield Raw Cotton
Pair each No. 2, No. 3 and No. 5 knitting needles
Cable needle

MEASUREMENTS
One size, to fit up to bust 40 in, 102 cm
Actual measurements — 53½ in, 136 cm
Length – 22 in, 56 cm
Sleeve length – 17 in, 43 cm

GAUGE
25 sts and 28 rows to 4 in (10 cm) over pat on No. 5 needles.

ABBREVIATIONS
alt – alternate; beg – beginning; c 6 – slip next 3 sts on to cable needle and hold at front, k 3 then k 3 from cable needle; cm – centimeters; cont – continue; dec –decrease; in – inches; inc – increase; k – knit; m 1 – make 1 st by picking up the strand between sts and k it through the back of the loop; p – purl; pat – pattern; rem – remaining rep – repeat; sl – slip; st(s) – stitch(es)

BACK
With No. 2 needles, cast on 147 sts.
1st row (right side) K 1, *p 1, k 1; rep from * to end.
2nd row P 1, *k 1, p 1; rep from * to end.
Rep these 2 rows for 1½ in (4 cm), ending with a right-side row.
Inc row Rib 2, *m 1, rib 6; rep from * to last st, m 1, rib 1. 172 sts.
Change to No. 5 needles.
Cont in pat thus:
1st row (right side) K 11, *p 6, k 18; rep from * to last 17 sts, p 6, k 11.
2nd and alt rows P 11, *k 6, p 18; rep from * to last 17 sts, k 6, p 11.
3rd row K 11, *p 6, c 6, k 12; rep from

* to last 17 sts, p 6, c 6, k 5.
5th, 7th and 9th rows As 1st row.
11th row As 3rd row.
13th, 15th and 17th rows As 1st row.
19th row As 3rd row.
21st row As 1st row.
23rd row K 5, c 6, *p 6, k 12, c 6; rep from * to last 17 sts, p 6, k 11.
25th, 27th and 29th rows As 1st row.
31st row As 23rd row.
33rd, 35th and 37th rows As 1st row.
39th row As 23rd row.
40th row As 2nd row.
These 40 rows form pat. **
Pat straight until back measures 20 in (51 cm), ending with a wrong-side row.

Neck Shaping
1st row Pat 68 sts, turn.
Keeping pat correct, cont on these sts only for 1st side and leave rem sts on a spare needle.
***Bind off 5 sts at beg of next row, 4 sts on the next alt row, 3 sts on the next alt row, 2 sts on the next alt row and 1 st on the next alt row. 53 sts. Work 6 rows straight.

Shoulder Shaping
Bind off 27 sts at beg of next row. Bind 1 row. Bind off rem 26 sts.
Next row With right side facing, sl center 36 sts on to a stitch holder, rejoin yarn to inner end of rem 68 sts. Complete to match 1st side from ***.

FRONT
Work as back to **.
Pat straight until front measures 22 rows less than back to shoulder, ending with a wrong-side row.

Neck Shaping
1st row Pat 68 sts, turn.
Keeping pat correct, cont on these sts only for 1st side and leave rem sts on a

spare needle.
****Bind off 4 sts at beg of next row, 3 sts on the next alt row, 2 sts on the next alt row. Dec 1 st at beg of foll 6 alt rows. Work 4 rows straight.

Shoulder Shaping
Work as back.
Next row As back.
Complete to match 1st side from ****.

SLEEVES
With No. 2 needles, cast on 63 sts.
Rib as back for 2 in (5 cm), ending with a right-side row.
Inc row Rib 2, *m 1, rib 5; rep from * to last st, m 1, rib 1. 76 sts.
Change to No. 5 needles.
Cont in pat thus:
1st row K 11, *p 6, k 18; rep from * to last 17 sts, p 6, k 11.
2nd row P 11, *k 6, p 18; rep from * to last 17 sts, k 6, p 11.
Cont in pat as set, inc 1 st each end of next and foll alt rows and working inc sts into pat, until there are 180 sts.
Pat 1 row. Bind off.

NECKBAND
Join right shoulder seam.
With with side facing, using No. 3 needles pick up and k 22 sts evenly down left front neck, k across 36 sts at center front, pick up and k 22 sts up right front neck, pick up and k 14 sts down right back neck, k across 36 sts of center back neck, pick up and k 14 sts up left back neck. 144 sts.
Work 1¼ in (3 cm) in k 1, p 1 rib. Bind off.

FINISHING
Join left shoulder and neckband seam. Sew on sleeves. Join side and sleeve seams. Press seams.

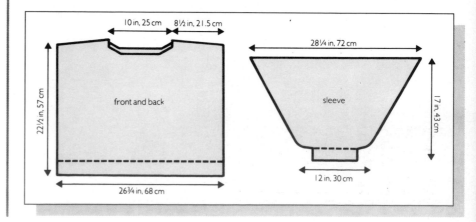

FIFTIES FOREVER

BE-BOP

BE-BOP

FIFTIES FOREVER

SILVER BEADS BLEND FIFTIES NOSTALGIA AND THE COWBOY CRAZE. THEY'RE SEWN ON TO A DECEPTIVELY DEMURE LITTLE CARDIGAN IN FINE WOOL. DESIGNED BY LESLEY STANFIELD

MATERIALS

8 (8, 9, 9) × 50 g balls King Cole Superwash 4 ply
Pair each No. 0 and No. 2 knitting needles
Sewing thread to match yarn
Beads: 10 × P10 (large round beads used as buttons), 200 × No 4 (small round beads), 210 × PO3 (oval beads), 12 g × M13-2 (bugle beads). Amounts are minimum quantities, except No 4 and PO3, all available from Ells & Farrier (see page 111).

MEASUREMENTS

To fit bust 32 (34, 36, 38) in, 81 (86, 91, 97) cm
Actual measurement – 33½ (35½, 37½, 39½) in, 85 (90, 95, 100) cm
Length – 21 (21¼, 22½, 23) in, 53 (54, 57, 58) cm
Sleeve length – 18 in, 46 cm
Figures in parenthesis are for larger sizes

GAUGE

32 sts and 40 rows to 4 in (10 cm) over st-st on No. 2 needles.

ABBREVIATIONS

alt – alternate; beg – beginning; cm – centimeters; cont – continue; dec – decrease; foll – following; in – inches; inc – increase; k – knit; p – purl; rem – remain(ing); rep – repeat; sl – slip; st(s) – stitch(es); st-st – stockinette stitch; tog – together
Work instructions in square brackets the number of times given

BACK

With No. 0 needles, cast on 138 (146, 154, 162) sts.

Work 48 rows in k 2, p 2 rib, beg wrong-side rows p 2.
Change to No. 2 needles and st-st. Work 96 (96, 104, 104) rows.

Armhole Shaping

Bind off 8 sts at beg of next 2 rows. Dec 1 st at each end of next row and every foll alt row until 110 (114, 118, 122) sts rem, thus ending with a k row. Work 63 rows straight, thus ending with a p row.

Shoulder Shaping

Bind off 8 (9, 10, 11) sts at beg of next 2 rows and 9 sts on the foll 6 rows. Leave rem 40 (42, 44, 46) sts on a stitch holder.

RIGHT FRONT

With No. 0 needles, cast on 79 (83, 87, 91) sts.
Work rib thus:
1st row K 7, sl 1, k 7, [p 2, k 2] to end.
2nd row [P 2, k 2] 16 (17, 18, 19) times, p 15.
Rep 1st and 2nd rows twice.
7th row (make buttonhole) K 2, bind off 3 sts, k 2 including st rem on needle after binding off, sl 1, k 2, bind off 3 sts, k 2 including st rem on needle after binding off, [p 2, k 2] to end.
8th row [P 2, k 2] 16 (17, 18, 19) times, p 2, cast on 3 sts, p 5, cast on 3 sts, p 2.
*Rep 1st and 2nd rows 9 times.
27th row As 7th.
28th row As 8th.
Rep from * once. (A total of 48 rows have been worked).
Change to No. 2 needles.
**Work main part thus:
1st row K 7, sl 1, k to end.
2nd row P.
Rep 1st and 2nd rows 9 (9, 10, 10) times.
21st (21st, 23rd, 23rd) row K 2, bind off 3 sts, k 2 including st rem on needle after binding off, sl 1, k 2, bind off 3 sts, k to end.
22nd (22nd, 24th, 24th) row P 66 (70, 74, 78), cast on 3 sts, p 5, cast on 3 sts, p 2.
Rep rows 1 to 22 (22, 24, 24) until a total of 97 (97, 105, 105) rows have been completed from **.

Armhole Shaping

Cont to work buttonholes with 20 (20, 22, 22) rows between, AND AT THE SAME TIME, bind off 8 sts at beg of next row, then dec 1 st at armhole

edge on the next 6 (8, 10, 12) right-side rows. 65 (67, 69, 71) sts.
Cont straight, working buttonholes as before, until the 16th (16th, 18th, 18th) row after the 9th buttonhole has been worked, thus ending with a p row.

Neck Shaping

Next row Sl 20 (21, 22, 23) sts on to a stitch holder, k 45 (46, 47, 48) sts.
Dec 1 st at neck edge on the next 10 rows. 35 (36, 37, 38) sts.
Work 14 (18, 16, 20) rows straight, thus ending with a k row.

Shoulder Shaping

Bind off 8 (9, 10, 11) sts at beg of next row and 9 sts on the foll 2 alt rows. Work 1 row. Bind off rem 9 sts.

LEFT FRONT

With No. 0 needles, cast on 79 (83, 87, 91) sts.
Work rib thus:
1st row [K 2, p 2] 16 (17, 18, 19) times, k 7, sl 1, k 7.
2nd row P 15, [k 2, p 2] to end.
Rep 1st and 2nd rows 23 times.
Change to No. 2 needles
Complete to match right front from **, omitting buttonholes.

SLEEVES

With No. 0 needles, cast on 70 (74, 78, 82) sts.
Rib 3 in (8 cm) as given at beg of back.
Change to No. 2 needles and cont in st-st.
Inc 1 st at each end of 1st row and every foll 8th (8th, 8th, 6th) row until there are 98 (106, 114, 122) sts.
Cont straight until sleeve measures 18 in, (46 cm) from cast-on edge, ending with a p row.

Cap Shaping

Bind off 8 sts at beg of next 2 rows. Dec 1 st at each end of every row until 66 (74, 82, 90) sts rem, then at each end of every 3rd row until 34 (40, 46, 52) sts rem.
Bind off 2 sts at beg of next 4 rows. 26 (32, 38, 44) sts.
Working k 2 (0, 2, 0), [k 2 tog, k 2] to end, bind off.

NECKBAND

Join shoulder seams.
With right side facing and using No. 0 needles, across sts of right front stitch holder work k 7, sl 1, k 12 (13,

14, 15), pick up and k 24 (28, 26, 30) sts up right front neck, k across 40 (42, 44, 46) sts of back neck, pick up and k 24 (28, 26, 30) sts down left front neck, then across sts on stitch holder work k 12 (13, 14, 15), sl 1, k 7. 128 (140, 140, 152) sts.

1st row P 15, k 2, [p 2, k 2] to last 15 sts, p 15.

2nd row K 7, sl 1, k 7, p 2, [k 2, p 2] to last 15 sts, k 7, sl 1, k 7.

3rd row As 1st.

4th row (buttonhole row) K 2, bind off 3 sts, k 2 including st rem on needle after binding off, sl 1, k 2, bind off 3 sts, k 2 including st rem on needle after binding off, rib to last 15 sts, k 7, sl 1, k 7.

5th row P 15, rib to last 15 sts, p 2, cast on 3 sts, p 5, cast on 3 sts, p 2.

6th row As 2nd.

7th row As 1st.

Rep 6th and 7th rows once. Bind off with sts as set.

FINISHING

Press. Sew on beads as diagram, using knitting yarn for all except bugle beads. Start with larger flower centers and work outwards. Match left front by using rows and sts as a guide to placing motifs. To make stems, thread bugle beads with sewing thread, lay on knitting, then couch down (ie take a small st over the sewing thread between each bead). Cont the random small beads at neck around back neck. Turn in front facings and sew down, then neaten ends. Neaten buttonholes. Set in sleeves easing in fullness at top. Join side and sleeve seams. Sew on size P 10 beads as buttons.

PATTERN FOR BEADWORK

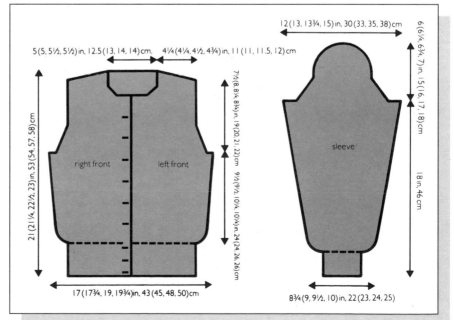

CLASSIC COLLECTION

CLASSIC COLLECTION

MARLBOROUGH

*M*ORE LIKE A VAST,
WARM COAT,
THIS OVER-SIZED
CARDIGAN HAS
KNOTTED CABLES, DEEP
RIBS AND SIDE
VENTS. DESIGNED BY
SUZANNE RUSSELL

MATERIALS
18 × 50 g balls Yarnworks Merino
Pair each No. 4 and No. 6 knitting
needles
Cable needle
5 buttons

MEASUREMENTS
One size, to fit up to bust 42 in, 107 cm
Actual measurement – 60 in, 153 cm
Length – 28¾ in, 73 cm
Sleeve length – 17¼ in, 44 cm

GAUGE
24 sts and 26 rows to 4 in (10 cm) over
pat on No. 6 needles

ABBREVIATIONS
beg – beginning; c 4 f – sl next 3 sts on
to cable needle and hold at front, p 1
then k 3 from cable needle; c 5 b – sl
next 2 sts on to cable needle and hold
at back, k 3 then p 2 from cable needle;
c 6 b – sl next 3 sts on to cable needle
and hold at back, k 3 then k 3 from
cable needle; c 6 f – sl next 3 sts on to
cable needle and hold at front, k 3 then
k 3 from cable needle; c 7 dec – sl next
3 sts on to cable needle and hold at
front, k 2 tog, k 1, p 1 then k 3 from
cable needle; cm – centimeters; cont –
continue; dec – decrease; d inc – work
k 1 tbl and k 1 into next st, take point of
left needle behind work and pick up
the strand between the base of the 2

sts just worked and k it tbl; foll –
following; in – inches; inc – increase; k –
knit; m 1 – make 1 st by picking up
strand between sts and k it tbl; p – purl;
pat – pattern; psso – pass slipped
stitch over; rem remain(ing); rep
repeat; sl – slip; sl 1 p – slip 1 purl-wise;
st(s) – stitch(es); tbl – through back of
loop(s); tog – together; wyif – with
yarn in front

NOTE
When working in pat the number of
sts varies from row to row where sts

are made and lost. When shaping do
not include these extra sts in any stitch
checks.

BACK
With No. 6 needles, cast on 190 sts
1st rib row (right side) K 2, *p 2, k 2;
rep from * to end.
2nd rib row P 2, *k 2, p 2; rep from *
to end.
Rep 1st and 2nd rib rows until back
measures 6¼ in (16 cm) from cast-on
edge, ending with a 1st rib row.
Dec row K 4, *k 2 tog, k 10; rep from *

M·A·R·L·B·O·R·O·U·G·H

14 times, k 2 tog, k 4. 174 sts.
Work foundation rows thus:
1st row (right side) P 2, *p 4, k 2, p 4; rep from * to last 2 sts, p 2.
2nd row K 2, *k 4, p 2, k 4; rep from * to last 2 sts, k 2.
3rd to 10th rows Rep 1st and 2nd rows 4 times.
Cont in pat thus:
1st row (right side) P 2, *p 4, k 2, p 5, d inc, p 2, k 2, p 4; rep from * to last 12 sts, p 4, k 2, p 6.
2nd row K 2, *k 4, p 2, k 8, p 2, k 2, p 3, k 1; rep from * to last 12 sts, k 4, p 2, k 6.
3rd row P 2, *p 4, k 2, p 5, c 4 f, p 1, k 2, p 2, d inc, p 1; rep from * to last 12 sts, p 4, k 2, p 6.
4th row K 2, *k 4, p 2, k 5, p 3, k 2, p 2, k 1, p 3, k 2; rep from * to last 12 sts, k 4, p 2, k 6.
5th row P 2, *p 4, k 2, p 6, c 4 f, m 1, k 2, c 5 b, p 1; rep from * to last 12 sts, p 4, k 2, p 6.
6th row K 2, *k 4, p 2, k 7, p 9, k 3; rep from * to last 12 sts, k 4, p 2, k 6.
7th row P 2, *p 4, k 2, p 7, c 6 b, k 3, p 3; rep from * to last 12 sts, p 4, k 2, p 6.
8th row As 6th.
9th row P 2, *p 4, k 2, p 7, k 3, c 6 f, p 3; rep from * to last 12 sts, p 4, k 2, p 6.
10th row As 6th.
11th row As 7th.
12th row As 6th.
13th row P 2, *p 4, k 2, p 5, c 5 b, c 7 dec, p 2; rep from * to last 12 sts, p 4, k 2, p 6.
14th row K 2, *k 4, p 2, k 6, p 3, k 1, p 2, k 2, wyif sl 1 p, p 2 tog, psso, k 1; rep from * to last 12 sts, k 4, p 2, k 6.
15th row P 2, *p 4, k 2, p 8, k 2, p 1, k 3, p 2; rep from * to last 12 sts, p 4, k 2, p 6.
16th row K 2, *k 4, p 2, k 6, wyif, sl 1 p, p 2 tog, psso, k 1, p 2, k 4; rep from * to last 12 sts, k 4, p 2, k 6.
17th row P 2, *p 4, k 2, p 4; rep from * to last 2 sts, p 2.
18th row K 2, *k 4, p 2, k 4; rep from * to last 2 sts, k 2.
19th row P 2, *p 1, d inc, p 2, k 2, p 8, k 2, p 4; rep from * to last 12 sts, p 1, d inc, p 2, k 2, p 6.
20th row K 2, *k 4, p 2, k 2, p 3, k 5, p 2, k 4; rep from * to last 14 sts, k 4, p 2, k 2, p 3, k 3.
21st row P 2, *p 1, c 4 f, p 1, k 2, p 2, d inc, p 5, k 2, p 4; rep from * to last 14 sts, p 1, c 4 f, p 1, k 2, p 2, d inc, p 3.

22nd row K 2, *k 1, p 3, k 2, p 2, k 1, p 3, k 6, p 2, k 4; rep from * to last 16 sts, k 1, p 3, k 2, p 2, k 1, p 3, k 4.
23rd row P 2, *p 2, c 4 f, m 1, k 2, c 5 b, p 5, k 2, p 4; rep from * to last 16 sts, p 2, c 4 f, m 1, k 2, c 5 b, p 3.
24th row K 2, *k 3, p 9, k 7, p 2, k 4; rep from * to last 17 sts, k 3, p 9, k 5.
25th row P 2, *p 3, c 6 b, k 3, p 7, k 2, p 4; rep from * to last 17 sts, p 3, c 6 b, k 3, p 5.
26th row As 24th.
27th row P 2, *p 3, k 3, c 6 f, p 7, k 2, p 4; rep from * to last 17 sts, p 3, k 3, c 6 f, p 5.
28th row As 24th.
29th row As 25th.
30th row As 24th.

31st row P 2, *p 1, c 5 b, c 7 dec, p 6, k 2, p 4; rep from * to last 17 sts, p 1, c 5 b, c 7 dec, p 4.
32nd row K 2, *k 2, p 3, k 1, p 2, k 2, wyif sl 1 p, p 2 tog, psso, k 5, p 2, k 4; rep from * to last 16 sts, k 2, p 3, k 1, p 2, k 2, wyif sl 1 p, p 2 tog, psso, k 3.
33rd row P 2, *p 4, k 2, p 1, k 3, p 6, k 2, p 4; rep from * to last 14 sts, p 4, k 2, p 1, k 3, p 4.
34th row K 2, *k 2, wyif sl 1 p, p 2 tog, psso, k 1, p 2, k 8, p 2, k 4; rep from * to last 14 sts, k 2, wyif sl 1 p, p 2 tog, psso, k 1, p 2, k 6.
35th row As 17th.
36th row As 18th.
These 36 rows form pat.
Rep 1st to 36th rows twice, then work

1st to 18th rows again.
Rep 17th and 18th rows.
Bind off loosely in pat.

POCKET LININGS

Make 2 With No. 6 needles, cast on 36 sts.
1st row K 1, *p 2, k 2; rep from * to last 3 sts, p 2, k 1.
2nd row P 1, *k 2, p 2; rep from * to last 3 sts, k 2, p 1.
Rep 1st and 2nd rows until work measures 6 in (15 cm) from cast-on edge, ending with a 1st row. Break off yarn and leave sts on a spare needle.

LEFT FRONT

With No. 6 needles, cast on 102 sts.
Work 1st and 2nd rib rows of back until rib measures same as back, ending with a 1st rib row.
Pocket Opening and dec row *K 6, k 2 tog; rep from * 3 times, k 1, sl next 36 sts on to a stitch holder, k across sts of one pocket lining, k 1, **k 2 tog, k 6; rep from ** 3 times. 94 sts.
Work the 10 foundation rows as back.
Cont in pat thus:
Work 19th to 36th rows, then 1st to 18th rows – thus pat will alternate with back at side seam.

Front Shaping

Keeping pat correct, beg with 19th row and dec 1 st at end of next row and at same edge on every foll 3rd row until 63 sts rem – note after working 36th row for 4th time, work 35th row again, thus last dec will be on this row. Work 36th row once more. Bind off loosely in pat.

RIGHT FRONT

Work as left front but work first front dec at beg of row.

LEFT SLEEVE

With No. 4 needles, cast on 50 sts.
Rib 3 in (8 cm) at beg of back, ending with a 1st rib row.
Inc row K 5, *inc in next st, k 12; rep from * twice, inc in next st, k 5. 54 sts.
Change to No. 6 needles.
Work 1st and 2nd foundation rows of back 3 times.
Beg with 19th row cont in pat as back, inc 1 st at each end of every wrong-side row until there are 134 sts, taking inc sts into pat.
Pat straight until sleeve measures 17¼ in (44 cm) from cast-on edge, ending with a wrong-side row.

Saddle Shaping

Bind off 55 sts at beg of next 2 rows. 24 sts.
Inc row K 3, p 2, *k 2, p twice in next st; rep from * once, k 2, **p twice in next st, k 2; rep from ** once, p 2, k 3. 28 sts.
Next row P 3, *k 2, p 2; rep from * to last st, p 1.
Next row (right side) K 3, *p 2, k 2; rep from * to last st, k 1.
Rep last 2 rows until saddle extension, when slightly stretched, will fit along front shoulder, ending with a right-side row***.
Next row Bind off 1 st, rib 18 including st rem on right needle after binding-off and sl these 18 sts on to a stitch holder, rib to end. Cont in rib on these 9 sts. Dec 1 st at inner end of the next 7

rows.
Rib rem 2 sts tog and fasten off securely.

RIGHT SLEEVE

Work as left sleeve to *** but end with a wrong-side row.
Complete to match left sleeve.

BUTTONHOLE BAND

Leaving center 44 sts of back free, join saddle extensions to bind-off edges of back and fronts, taking 1 st from each edge of extensions into seam.
With right side facing and using No. 1 needles, pick up and k 88 sts evenly up right front edge to beg of front shaping and 76 sts up remainder of front to saddle extension, rib across 18 sts on stitch holder, then pick up and k 27 sts evenly to center back neck, turn and cast on 1 st. 210 sts.
Beg with 2nd rib row of back, rib 5 rows.
1st buttonhole row (right side) Rib 3, bind off next 3 sts, *rib 17 sts including st rem on needle after binding off, bind off next 3 sts; rep from *3 times, rib to end.
2nd buttonhole row Rib to end binding on 3 sts over each bind-off group of 1st row.
Rib 6 rows.
Bind off in rib.

BUTTON BAND

Work to match buttonhole band, casting on the 1st at beg of pick up row and omitting buttonholes.

FINISHING

Join front bands at center back neck taking 1 st from each edge into seam. With wrong side facing sl 36 sts of pocket on to a No. 6 needle and bind off knit-wise. Leaving ribs open, join side seams to within 9 in (23 cm) of bind-off edges of back and fronts. Join sleeve seams. Sew bind-off edges of sleeves into armholes. Sew down pocket linings on wrong side. Sew on buttons.

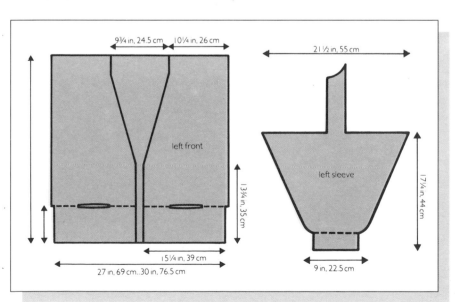

9¾ in, 24.5 cm · 10¼ in, 26 cm · 21½ in, 55 cm · left front · 13¾ in, 35 cm · left sleeve · 17¼ in, 44 cm · 15¼ in, 39 cm · 27 in, 69 cm...30 in, 76.5 cm · 9 in, 22.5 cm

MARLBOROUGH

CLASSIC COLLECTION

WINCHESTER

A HUSKY FAIR ISLE IN MUTED NATURAL COLORS BLENDS PERFECTLY WITH COUNTRY CLOTHES – AND WOULD LOOK JUST AS GOOD ON A MAN. DESIGNED BY TESSA DENNISON

MATERIALS

Emu Harlech DK Welsh Wool
6 (7) × 50 g balls Bangor (M)
5 (5) × 50 g balls Raglan (A)
5 (6) × 50 g balls Snowdon (B)
2 (2) × 50 g balls Anglesey (C)
Pair each No. 3 and No. 6 knitting needles

MEASUREMENTS

To fit bust 34-36 (38-40) in, 86-91 (97-102) cm
Actual measurement – 42½ (49) in, 108 (124) cm
Length – 25¼ (26) in, 64 (66) cm
Sleeve length – 17¼ in, 44 cm
Figures in parenthesis are for larger size

GAUGE

24 sts and 24 rows to 4 in (10 cm) measured over pat on No. 6 needles

ABBREVIATIONS

alt – alternate; beg – beginning; cm – centimeters; cont – continue; dec – decreas(e)(ing); foll – following; in – inches; inc – increas(e)(ing); k – knit; m 1 – make 1 st by picking up the strand between sts and k it through the back of the loop; p – purl; pat – pattern; rem – remain(ing); rep – repeat; sl – slip; st(s) – stitch(es); st-st – stockinette stitch

BACK

With No. 3 needles and A, cast on 130 (150) sts.
1st rib row (right side) K 2, *p 2, k 2; rep from * to end.
Break off A; join M.
2nd rib row P 2, *k 2, p 2; rep from * to end.

With M, rep 1st and 2nd rib rows until back measures 3 (4) in, 8 (10) cm from cast-on edge, ending with a 2nd rib row and inc 1 st at center of last row. 131 (151) sts. Change to No. 6 needles.
Cont in st-st from chart, carrying color not in use loosely across wrong side on two-color rows thus:
1st row (right side) Reading row 1 of chart from right to left, k 20 pat sts 6 (7) times, then k last 11 sts of chart.
2nd row Reading row 2 of chart from left to right, p first 11 sts of chart, then p 20 pat sts 6 (7) times.
3rd to 32nd rows As 1st and 2nd rows but working rows 3 to 32 of chart.
Rep these 32 rows 3 times.

Neck Shaping

Cont from chart taking care to keep pat correct.
1st row Pat 49 (59) sts, turn.
Cont on these sts only for 1st side and leave rem sts on a spare needle.
Bind off 3 sts at beg of next row and on

the foll alt row.
Cont in A. K 1 row. Bind off 3 sts at beg of next row.
Bind off rem 40 (50) sts.
Next row With right side facing, sl center 33 sts on to a stitch holder, rejoin yarn to inner end of rem 49 (59) sts and pat to end.
Pat 1 row.
Bind off 3 sts at beg of next row.
Pat 1 row.
Cont in A.
Bind off 3 sts at beg of next row and on the foll alt row.
Bind off rem 40 (50) sts.

FRONT

Work as back until the 32 rows of chart have been worked 3 times, then work rows 1 to 16 again.

Neck Shaping

1st row Pat 54 (64) sts, turn.
Cont on these sts only for 1st side and leave rem sts on a spare needle.

begin here

KEY

| B | A | M | C |

pattern

W·I·N·C·H·E·S·T·E·R

Bind off 3 sts at beg of next row and on the foll 2 alt rows.

Dec 1 st at neck edge on every alt row until 40 (50) sts rem.

Pat straight until front matches back to shoulder.

Bind off.

Next row: With right side facing, sl center 23 sts on to a stitch holder, rejoin yarn to inner end of rem 54 (64) sts and pat to end.

Pat 1 row.

Complete to match 1st side.

SLEEVES

With No. 3 needles and A, cast on 54 (58) sts.

Rib 1 row as back.

Break off A; join M.

Cont in rib until sleeve measures 3 in (8 cm) from cast-on edge, ending with a 1st rib row.

Next row Rib 3 (5), m 1, *rib 3 (4), m 1; rep from * to last 3 (5) sts, rib 3 (5). 71 sts.

Change to No.6 needles.

Cont in pat from chart as for back, working the 20 pat sts 3 times and inc 1 st at each end of every 4th row until there are 111 sts, working inc sts into pat. Pat straight until row 21 of chart has been worked for the 3rd time from top of rib. P 1 row with A.

Bind off loosely with A.

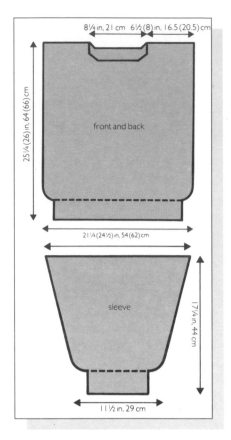

NECKBAND

Join right shoulder seam.

1st row With right side facing, using No. 3 needles and A, pick up and k 31 sts evenly down left front neck, k across 23 sts on stitch holder, pick up and k 31 sts up right front neck and 12 sts down right back neck, k across 33 sts on stitch holder then pick up and k 12 sts up left back neck. 142 sts.

2nd row P 1 A, reading row 18 of chart from left to right, p 20 pat sts 7 times, p 1 A.

3rd row K 1 A, reading row 19 of chart from right to left, k 20 pat sts 7 times, k 1 A.

4th row As 2nd row but working row 20 of chart.

5th row K with A.

Change to M and p 1 row.

Rib 6 rows as at beg of back.

Change to A and rib 2 rows.

Bind off evenly in rib.

FINISHING

Press pieces omitting rib. Join left shoulder and neckband seam. Place markers on side edges of back and front on row 16 of the 3rd rep of chart. With center of bind-off edge of sleeves to shoulder seams, sew on sleeves between markers. Join side and sleeve seams.

ETON

THE FISHERMAN'S GUERNSEY GOES SOFT IN CORAL RED COTTON. IT HAS ALL THE EASY FIT OF A SAILING SMOCK. DESIGNED BY SUE TURTON

MATERIALS

19 × 50 g balls Scheepjeswol
Mayflower Helarsgarn
Pair each No. 4 and No. 5 knitting
needles
Cable needle

MEASUREMENTS

One size, to fit up to bust 40 in, 102 cm
Actual measurement – 47½ in, 121 cm
Length – 27½ in, 70 cm
Sleeve length – 16½ in, 42 cm

GAUGE

19 sts and 29 rows to 4 in (10 cm) over
pat of Chart 2 using No. 5 needles

ABBREVIATIONS

beg – beginning; cm – centimeters;
cont – continue; dec – decrease; foll –
following; g-st – garter stitch; in –
inches; inc – increase; k – knit; m-st –
moss stitch; p – purl; pat – pattern;
rem – remaining; rep – repeat; sl – slip;
st(s) – stitch(es)

BACK AND FRONT ALIKE

With No. 4 needles, cast on 119 sts
using thumb method.
Work 6 rows in g-st.
Inc row K 6, *inc in next st, k 52; rep
from * once, inc in next st, k 6. 122 sts.
Change to No. 5 needles.
Cont in pat thus:
1st row (right side) K 3, *reading row
1 of Chart 1 from right to left work 8
sts, reading row 1 of Chart 2 from right
to left work 46 sts; rep from * once,
reading row 1 of Chart 1 from right to
left work 8 sts, k 3.
2nd row K 3, *reading row 2 of Chart
1 from left to right work 8 sts, reading
row 2 of Chart 2 from left to right
work 46 sts; rep from * once, reading

row 2 of Chart 1 from left to right
work 8 sts, k 3.
Cont in this way until a total of 190
rows of pat have been worked – note
that Chart 1 has 10 rows and Chart 2
has 38 rows; when 10 rows of pat
have been worked, cont with row 11
of Chart 2 but beg again at row 1 of
Chart 1.

Neck Shaping

Cont in g-st.
1st row K 44 sts, turn.
Cont on these sts only for 1st side.
Dec 1 st at neck edge on the next
4 rows. 40 sts.

K 1 row. Bind off.
Next row With right side facing, sl
center 34 sts on to a stitch holder,
rejoin yarn to inner end of rem 44 sts
and k to end.
Complete to match 1st side.

SLEEVES

With No. 4 needles, cast on 53 sts
using thumb method.
Work 6 rows in g-st.
Inc row K 26, inc in next st, k 26. 54 sts.
Change to No. 5 needles
Cont in pat thus:
1st row (right side) Reading row 1 of
Chart 2 from right to left work sts 1 to

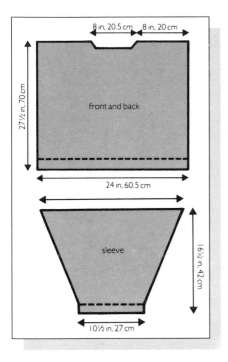

23, reading row 1 of Chart 1 from right to left work 8 sts, reading row 1 of Chart 2 from right to left work sts 24 to 46.

2nd row Reading row 2 of Chart 2 from left to right work sts 46 to 24,

reading row 2 of Chart 1 from left to right work 8 sts, reading row 2 of Chart 2 from left to right work sts 23 to 1.

Pat 2 rows.

Cont in this way, inc 1 st at each end of next row and every foll 4th row until there are 110 sts, working inc sts into moss-st (thus last st of row 6 should be k).

Pat 1 row, thus a total of 114 rows of pat have been worked.

P 1 row.

Bind off loosely knitwise.

NECKBAND

Join right shoulder seam using a flat seam.

With right side facing and using No. 4 needles, pick up and k 9 sts down left front neck, k across 34 sts at center front, pick up and k 9 sts up right front neck and 9 sts down right back neck, k across 34 sts at center back then pick up and k 9 sts up left back neck. 104 sts.

Work 19 rows in g-st. Bind off loosely.

FINISHING

Use flat seams throughout. Join left

shoulder and neckband seam. Fold neckband in half on to wrong side and whip stitch loosely in place. With center of bind-off edge of sleeves to shoulder seams, sew on sleeves. Join side and sleeve seams. Press seams.

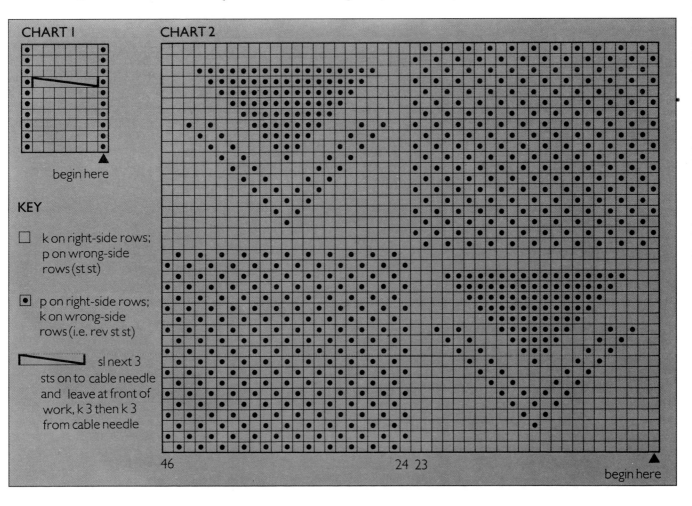

CHART 1

begin here

KEY

☐ k on right-side rows;
 p on wrong-side
 rows (st st)

⊡ p on right-side rows;
 k on wrong-side
 rows (i.e. rev st st)

◣ sl next 3
sts on to cable needle
and leave at front of
work, k 3 then k 3
from cable needle

CHART 2

46   24 23   begin here

ETON

CLASSIC COLLECTION

HARROW

A WELL-BRED SWEATER IN A SUBTLY UNTRADITIONAL YARN HAS BEAUTIFUL PROPORTIONS AND LEAFY STITCH DETAIL. DESIGNED BY AILEEN SWAN

MATERIALS
8 (9, 9) × 50 g balls Schachenmayr Stella
Pair each No. 1 and No. 3 knitting needles
Cable needle
Shoulder pads

MEASUREMENTS
To fit bust 32 (34, 36) in, 81 (86, 91) cm
Actual measurement – 33 1/2 (36, 38) in, 85 (91, 97) cm
Length – 21 1/4 in, 54 cm
Sleeve length – 17 3/4 in, 45 cm
Figures in parenthesis are for larger sizes

GAUGE
Based on a st-st gauge of 24 sts and 32 rows to 4 in (10 cm) on No. 4 needles, 30 sts of chart measure 4 1/4 in (10.5 cm)

ABBREVIATIONS
alt – alternate; beg – beginning; cm – centimeters; cont – continue; dec – decrease; foll – following; in – inches; inc – increase; k – knit; p – purl; pat – pattern; rem – remain(ing); rep – repeat; sl – slip; st(s) – stitch(es); st-st – stockinette stitch; tbl – through back of loop; tog – together
Work instructions in square brackets the number of times given

BACK
With No. 1 needles, cast on 105 (113, 121) sts.
1st rib row (right side) K 1 tbl, *p 1, k 1 tbl; rep from * to end.
2nd rib row P 1 tbl, *k 1, p 1 tbl; rep from * to end.
Rep 1st and 2nd rib rows 9 times, then work 1st rib row again.

Inc row K 1, inc in next st, *p 1 tbl, [inc in next st, p 1 tbl] 2 (3, 4) times, rib 6, inc in next st, [rib 3, inc in next st] twice, rib 12; rep from * twice, p 1 tbl, [inc in next st, p 1 tbl] 2 (3, 4) times, inc in next st, k 1. 124 (136, 148) sts.
Change to No. 3 needles.
Cont in pat thus:
1st row (right side) P 3, *k 1 tbl, [p 2, k 1 tbl] 2 (3, 4) times, reading row 1 of chart from right to left work 30 sts; rep from * twice, k 1 tbl, [p 2, k 1 tbl] 2 (3, 4) times, p 3.
2nd row K 3, *p 1 tbl, [k 2, p 1 tbl] 2 (3, 4) times, reading row 2 of chart from left to right work 30 sts; rep from * twice, p 1 tbl, [k 2, p 1 tbl] 2 (3, 4) times, k 3.
These 2 rows establish rib pat between and at each side of chart panels.
Cont in this way until each chart row has been worked.
These 36 rows from pat.
Cont in pat until row 20 (18, 16) of the 3rd pat from beg has been worked.

Armhole Shaping
Keeping pat correct, bind off 7 (9, 11) sts at beg of next 2 rows.
Dec 1 st at each end of next row and on the foll 4 (5, 6) alt rows. 100 (106, 112) sts**.
Pat straight until row 8 of the 5th pat from beg has been worked.

Shoulder and Neck Shaping
1st row Bind off 8 (9, 10) sts, pat until there are 28 (29, 30) sts on right needle, turn. Cont on these sts only leaving rem sts on a spare needle.
2nd row Bind off 5 sts, pat to end.
3rd row Bind off 8 (9, 10) sts, pat to end.
4th row As 2nd.
Bind off rem 10 sts.
Next row With right side facing, sl center 28 (30, 32) sts on to a stich holder, rejoin yarn to inner end of rem 36 (38, 40) sts and pat to end.
Bind off 8 (9, 10) sts at beg of next row.
Beg with 2nd row, complete to match 1st side.

FRONT
Work as back to **.
Pat straight until row 18 of the 4th pat from beg has been worked.

Neck Shaping
1st row Pat 39 (41, 43) sts, turn.

Cont on these sts only leaving rem sts on a spare needle.
***Bind off 2 sts at beg of next row and on the foll 3 alt rows. Dec 1 st at beg of next 5 alt rows. 26 (28, 30) sts.
Pat 8 rows straight.

Shoulder Shaping
Bind off 8 (9, 10) sts at beg of next row and on the foll alt row.
Pat 1 row. Bind off rem 10 sts.
Next row With right side facing, sl center 22 (24, 26) sts on to a stitch holder, rejoin yarn to inner end of rem 39 (41, 43) sts and pat to end.
Pat 1 row.
Complete to match 1st side from ***.

SLEEVES
With No. 1 needles, cast on 49 (53, 57) sts.
Rib 19 (21, 23) rows as at beg of back.
Inc row K 1, [inc in next st, p 1 tbl] 5 (6, 7) times, rib 6, inc in next st, [rib 3, inc in next st] twice, rib 12, [p 1 tbl, inc in next st] 5 (6, 7) times, k 1. 62 (68, 74) sts.
Change to No. 3 needles.
Cont in pat thus:
1st row (right side) P 3, k 1 tbl, [p 2, k 1 tbl] 4 (5, 6) times, reading from right to left work 30 sts of row 1 of chart, [k 1 tbl, p 2] 4 (5, 6) times, k 1 tbl, p 3.
2nd row K 3, p 1 tbl, [k 2, p 1 tbl] 4 (5, 6) times, reading from left to right work 30 sts of row 2 of chart, [p 1 tbl, k 2] 4 (5, 6) times, p 1 tbl, k 3.
Cont in pat in this way, inc 1 st at each end of 5th row and every foll 8th row until there are 86 (92, 98) sts, taking inc sts into rib at each side.
Pat straight until row 20 (18, 16) of the 4th pat from beg has been worked.

Cap Shaping
Bind off 7 (9, 11) sts at beg of next 2 rows. Dec 1 st at each end of next row and every foll alt row until 56 sts rem.
Dec 1 st at each end of every 4th row until 44 sts rem. Dec 1 st at each end of every row until 30 sts rem.
Next row P 2 tog to end.
Next row *K 1, k 2 tog; rep from * to end.
Bind off rem 10 sts.

NECKBAND
Join right shoulder seam.
With right side facing and using No. 1 needles, pick up and k 31 (32, 31) sts evenly down left front neck, across

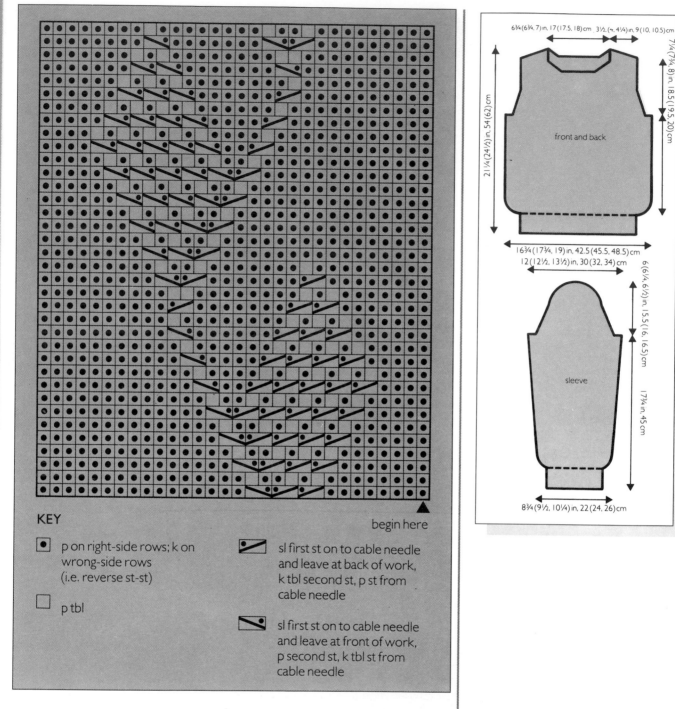

KEY

| ● | p on right-side rows; k on wrong-side rows (i.e. reverse st-st) |
| □ | p tbl |

sl first st on to cable needle and leave at back of work, k tbl second st, p st from cable needle

sl first st on to cable needle and leave at front of work, p second st, k tbl st from cable needle

begin here

center sts work, p 13 (14, 15), k 1 tbl, p 2 tog, k 1 tbl, p 5 (6, 7); pick up and k 31 (32, 31) sts up right front neck and 15 (14, 15) sts down right back neck; across center sts work, p 4 (5, 6) [k 1 tbl, p 1] 4 times, k 1 tbl, p 2 tog, k 1 tbl, p 12 (13, 14); pick up and k 15 (14, 15) sts up left back neck then cast on 1 st for seam. 141 (145, 149) sts. Beg with 2nd rib row, rib 2½ in (6 cm) as at beg of back. Bind off very loosely in rib.

FINISHING
Join left shoulder and neckband seam.

Fold neckband in half on to wrong side and whipstitch loosely in place. Set in sleeves. Taking 1½ sts from each edge into seams, join side and sleeve seams. Sew in shoulder pads.

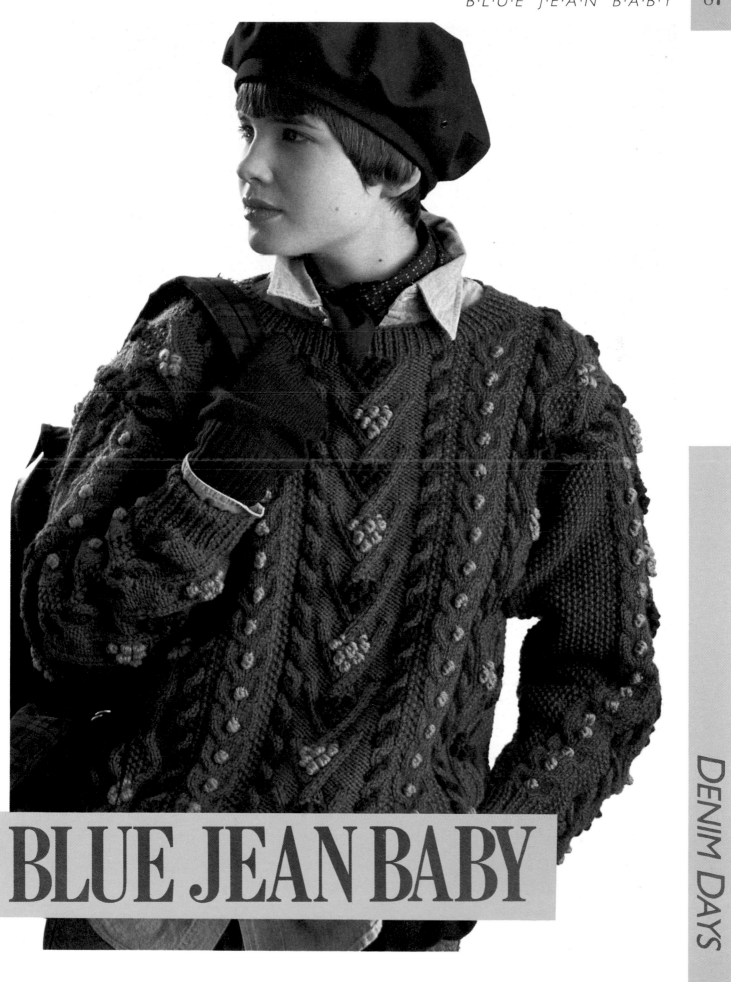

BLUE JEAN BABY

DENIM DAYS

STORMY SKY COLOURS AND DENSE ARAN STITCHES COMBINE TO PRODUCE A RUGGED OUTDOOR SWEATER, DESTINED TO BECOME A FUTURE CLASSIC. DESIGNED BY CAROLINE INGRAM

MATERIALS
Robin Pure New Wool Aran:
17 × 50 g balls shade Danube (M)
3 × 50 g balls shade Marine (A)
2 × 50 g balls shade Como (B)
Pair each No. 4 and No. 6 knitting needles
Cable needle

MEASUREMENTS
One size, to fit up to bust 38 in, 97 cm
Actual measurement – 42 in, 106 cm approx
Length – 24 in, 61 cm approx
Sleeve length – 17 in, 43 cm approx

GAUGE
20 sts and 30 rows to 4 in (10 cm) measured over m-st on No. 6 needles

ABBREVIATIONS
alt – alternate; beg – beginning; c 4 b – slip next 2 sts on to cable needle and hold at back, k 2 then k 2 from cable needle; c 4 f – slip next 2 sts on to cable needle and hold at front, k 2 then k 2 from cable needle; c 3 b – slip next st on to cable needle and hold at back, k 2 then p st from cable needle; c 3 f – slip next 2 sts on to cable needle and hold at front of work, p 1 then k 2 from cable needle; c 5 b – slip next 3 sts on to cable needle and hold at back, k 2, slip last st from cable needle to left hand needle and p this st, then k 2 from cable needle; cm – centimeters; cont – continue; dec – decrease; foll – following; in – inches; inc – increase; k – knit; m 1 – make 1 st by picking up the strand between sts and k it through the back of the loop; m b – make bobble by working [k 1, p 1] 3 times, k 1 into next st (7 sts), then pass 2nd, 3rd, 4th,

5th, 6th, 7th sts over 1st st; m-st – moss stitch; pat – pattern; p – purl; rem – remaining; rep – repeat; sl – slip; st(s) – stitch(es); tog – together

BACK
With No. 4 needles and M, cast on 113 sts.
1st row (right side) P 1, *k 1, p 1; rep from * to end.
2nd row K 1, *p 1, k 1; rep from * to end.
Rep these 2 rows 7 times, then work 1st row again.
Inc row Rib 2, m 1, rib 4, m 1, rib 6, m 1, rib 13, m 1, rib 4, m 1, rib 7, m 1, rib 7, m 1, rib 6, m 1, rib 15, m 1, rib 6, m 1, rib 7, m 1, rib 7, m 1, rib 4, m 1, rib 13, m 1, rib 6, m 1, rib 4, m 1, rib 2. 129 sts.
Change to No. 6 needles.
Cont in pat thus, using M except where indicated otherwise and twisting yarns at color changes:
1st row (right side) [K 1, p 1] 5 times, work 1st row of panel 1, work 1st row of panel 2, work 1st row of panel 3, [p 1, k 1] twice, **work 1st row of panel 4, [k 1, p 1] twice, work 1st row of

panel 1, work 1st row of panel 5, work 1st row of panel 3, [p 1, k 1] twice, work 1st row of panel 4, **[k 1, p 1] twice, work 1st row of panel 1, work 1st row of panel 2, work 1st row of panel 3, [p 1, k 1] 5 times.
2nd row [K 1, p 1] 4 times, k 2, work 2nd row of panel 3, work 2nd row of panel 2, work 2nd row of panel 1, k 2, p 1, k 1, **work 2nd row of panel 4, k 1, p 1, k 2, work 2nd row of panel 3, work 2nd row of panel 5, work 2nd row of panel 1, k 2, p 1, k 1, work 2nd row of panel 4, **k 1, p 1, k 2, work 2nd row of panel 3, work 2nd row of panel 2, work 2nd row of panel 1, k 2, [p 1, k 1] 4 times.
These 2 rows set position of panels and m-st.
Cont to pat as set from 3rd row of panels. Rep each panel as it is completed.
Pat straight until work measures 15 in (38 cm) approx, ending with 14th row of 4th rep of panel 5.

Armhole Shaping
Bind off 8 sts at beg of next 2 rows.

113 sts. ***
Keeping pat correct, cont straight until back measures 24 in (61 cm) approx, ending with last row of 6th rep of panel 5.
Next row Bind off 29 sts, sl next 55 sts on to a stitch holder, rejoin yarn to inner end of rem 29 sts.
Bind off.

FRONT

Work as back to ***.
Keeping pat correct, cont straight until front measures 20 in (51 cm) approx, ending with 24th row of 5th rep of panel 5.

Neck Shaping

1st row Pat 46, turn.
Cont on these sts only for 1st side and leave rem sts on a spare needle.
Dec 1 st at neck edge on next 17 rows. 29 sts.
Pat 14 rows straight.
Bind off.
Next row With right side facing, sl center 21 sts on to a stitch holder, rejoin yarn to inner end of rem 46 sts and pat to end.
Complete to match 1st side.

SLEEVES

Using No. 4 needles and M, cast on 45 sts.
Work 17 rows rib as for back.
Inc row (wrong side) Rib 3, *m 1, rib 3; rep from * to end. 59 sts.
Change to No. 6 needles.
Cont in pat thus, using M except where indicated otherwise:
1st row P 1, k 1, work from ** to ** of 1st row of back, k 1, p 1.
2nd row P 1, k 1, work from ** to ** of 2nd row of back, k 1, p 1.
These 2 rows set position of panels and m-st.
Cont in pat as set, AT THE SAME TIME inc 1 st at each end of next and foll 4th rows, working extra sts in m-st, until there are 105 sts.
Pat straight until sleeve measures 18½ in (47 cm) approx, ending with 14th row of 5th rep of panel 5.
Bind off.

NECKBAND

Join right shoulder seam.
With No. 4 needles and M, pick up and k 27 sts evenly down left front neck, k 10, k 2 tog, k 9 across 21 sts at center front, pick up and k 27 sts up right front neck then k 13, *k 2 tog,

k 12; rep from * to end across 55 sts of back neck. 126 sts.
Work 9 rows k 1, p 1 rib. Bind off in rib.

FINISHING

Join left shoulder and neckband seam. With center of bind-off edge of sleeves to shoulder seams and straight edges of sleeves to bind-off sts at armholes, set in sleeves. Join side and sleeve seams. Press seams.

PANEL 1 (4 sts)
1st row K 2, k 2 A.
2nd row P 2 A, p 2.
3rd row C 4 b, working colors as set.
4th row P 2, p 2 A.
5th row K 2 A, k 2.
6th row As 4th.
7th row C 4 b, working colors as set.
8th row As 2nd.

PANEL 2 (15 sts)
1st row P 5, k 2, m b A, k 2, p 5.
2nd row K 5, p 5, k 5.
3rd row P 5, [k 1, m b A] twice, k 1, p 5.
4th row As 2nd.
5th row As 1st.
6th row As 2nd.
7th row P 4, c 3 b, p 1, c 3 f, p 4.
8th row K 4, p 2, k 1, p 1, k 1, p 2, k 4.
9th row P 3, c 3 b, k 1, p 1, k 1, c 3 f, p 3.
10th row K 3, p 3, k 1, p 1, k 1, p 3, k 3.
11th row P 2, c 3 b, [p 1, k 1] twice, p 1, c 3 f, p 2.
12th row K 2, p 2, [k 1, p 1] 3 times, k 1, p 2, k 2.
13th row P 2, k 3, [p 1, k 1] twice, p 1, k 3, p 2.
14th row K 2, p 2, [k 1, p 1] 3 times, k 1, p 2, k 2.
15th row P 2, c 3 f, [p 1, k 1] twice, p 1, c 3 b, p 2.
16th row K 3, p 3, k 1, p 1, k 1, p 3, k 3.
17th row P 3, c 3 f, k 1, p 1, k 1, c 3 b, p 3.
18th row K 4, p 2, k 1, p 1, k 1, p 2, k 4.
19th row P 4, c 3 f, p 1, c 3 b, p 4.
20th row K 5, p 5, k 5.
21st to 40th rows Rep 1st to 20th rows but work bobbles with B.

PANEL 3 (4 sts)
1st row K 2, k 2 A.
2nd row P 2 A, p 2.
3rd row C 4 f, working colors as set.
4th row P 2, p 2 A.
5th row K 2 A, k 2.
6th row As 4th.
7th row C 4 f, working colors as set.
8th row As 2nd.

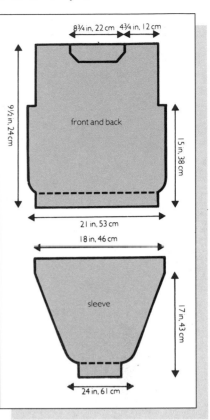

PANEL 4 (9 sts)
1st row K 9.
2nd row P 9.
3rd row C 4 b, k 1, c 4 f.
4th row P 9.
5th row K 4, m b B, k 4.
6th row P 9.
7th and 8th rows As 1st and 2nd rows.

PANEL 5 (21 sts)
1st row P 8, c 5 b, p 8.
2nd row K 8, p 2, k 1, p 2, k 8.
3rd row P 7, c 3 b, p 1, c 3 f, p 7.
4th row K 7, p 2, k 3, p 2, k 7.
5th row P 6, c 3 b, p 1, m b B, p 1, c 3 f, p 6.
6th row K 6, p 2, k 5, p 2, k 6.
7th row P 5, c 3 b, [p 1, m b B] twice, p 1, c 3 f, p 5.
8th row K 5, p 2, k 7, p 2, k 5.
9th row P 4, c 3 b, [p 1, m b B] 3 times, p 1, c 3 f, p 4.
10th row K 4, p 2, k 9, p 2, k 4.
11th row P 3, c 3 b, p 2, k 2, p 1, k 2, p 2, c 3 f, p 3.
12th row [K 3, p 2] twice, k 1, [p 2, k 3] twice.
13th row P 2, c 3 b, p 3, k 2, p 1, k 2, p 3, c 3 f, p 2.
14th row K 2, p 2, k 4, p 2, k 1, p 2, k 4, p 2, k 2.
15th to 28th rows Rep 1st to 14th rows but work bobbles with A.

TURKESTAN

BOKHARA

AN EXOTIC COMBINATION OF RICH COLOR AND FOLK-INSPIRED PATTERNS, THIS HUGE MOHAIR SWEATER IS ALMOST A TUNIC, TAPERING TO A BROAD BAND AT THE HIP. DESIGNED BY MELODY GRIFFITHS

MATERIALS
Sunbeam Paris Mohair:
11 × 25 g balls shade Electric (M)
11 × 25 g balls shade Storm (A)
5 × 25 g balls shade Sunshade (B)
2 × 25 g balls shade Neptune (C)
1 × 25 g ball shade Gold Dust (D)
Pair each No. 7 and No. 8 knitting needles

MEASUREMENTS
One size, to fit up to 38 in, 97 cm
Actual measurement – 47½ in, 121 cm
Length – 29 in, 74 cm
Sleeve length – 18½ in, 47 cm

GAUGE
17 sts and 17 rows to 4 in (10 cm) measured over pat on No. 8 needles

ABBREVIATIONS
beg – beginning; cm – centimeters; cont – continue; dec – decrease; foll – following; in – inches; inc – increase; k – knit; p – purl; pat – pattern; rem – remaining; sl – slip; st(s) – stitch(es); st-st – stockinette stich; tog – together

NOTE
This garment uses three methods of

working with color.
Charts 1 and 3 are worked in traditional Fair Isle technique. Charts 2 and 4 are worked in a combination of Fair Isle for shades Electric and Storm with motif knitting for Sunshade and Neptune. Do not carry Sunshade and Neptune all the way across back of work. The single Gold Dust sts are duplicate stitch after pieces are completed – they should be knitted in Storm
Charts 2 and 4 are in two halves; in each case the two halves should be read as one.

BACK
With No. 8 needles and A, cast on 27 sts for hip band.
Work in st–st from Chart 1 thus:
1st row is a k row, read chart from right to left.
2nd row is a p row, read chart from left to right.
Cont from chart in this way until all 81 rows have been worked.
Bind off purl-wise with A.
With right side facing, join A to 1st st of 1st row then pick up and k 83 sts evenly along row-ends of hip band to cast-on edge.
Work in st-st from Chart 2 thus:
1st row is a p row, read chart from left to right.
2nd row is a k row, read chart from right to left.

B·O·K·H·A·R·A

CHART I

CHART 2

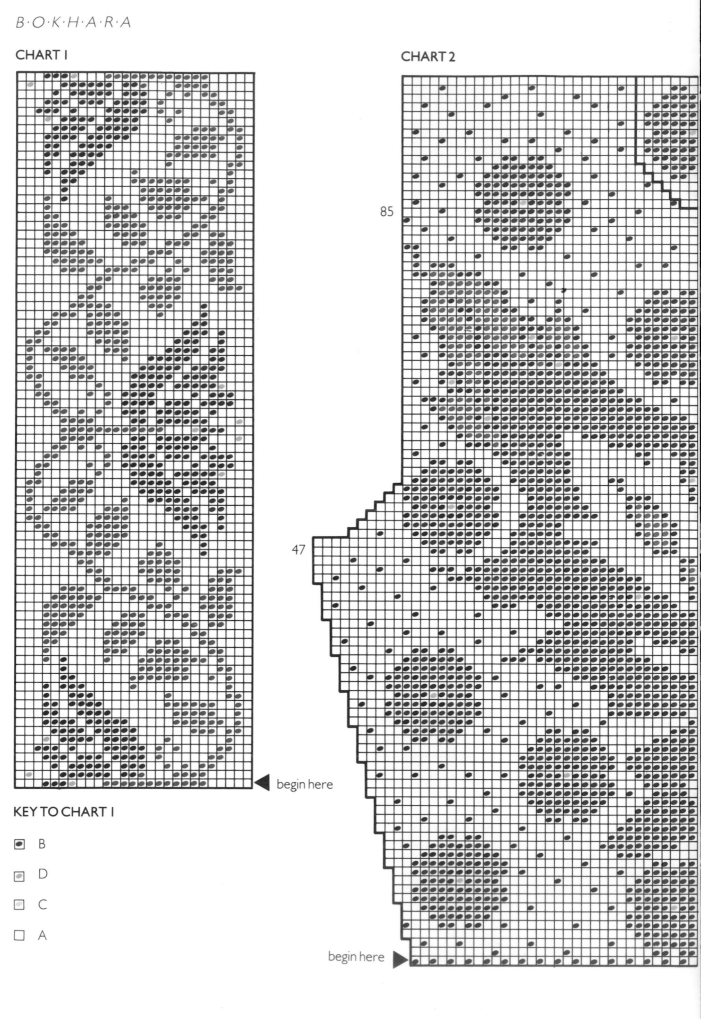

begin here

KEY TO CHART I

- ◉ B
- ▨ D
- ◻ C
- ☐ A

85

47

begin here ▶

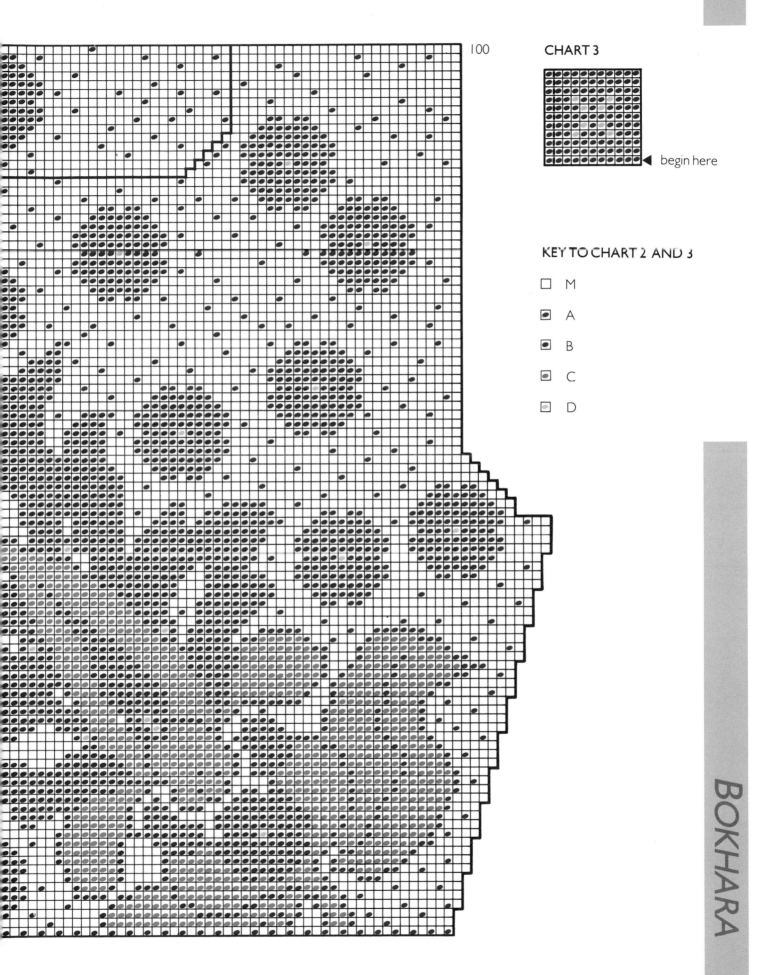

100

CHART 3

◄ begin here

KEY TO CHART 2 AND 3

☐ M

▣ A

▣ B

▣ C

▣ D

B·O·K·H·A·R·A

CHART 4

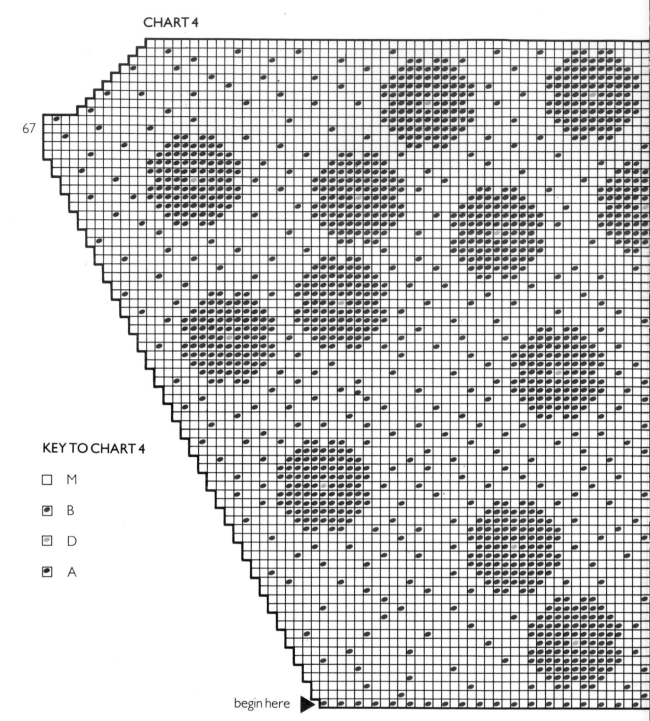

67

begin here ▶

KEY TO CHART 4

☐   M

▣   B

▣   D

▣   A

Cont from chart in this way, inc 1 st at each end of 4th row of chart and every foll 4th row as shown, until there are 105 sts.
Pat 3 rows straight, thus completing 47 rows of chart.

Armhole Shaping
Cont from chart, binding off 4 sts at beg of next 2 rows.
Dec 1 st at each end of next 6 rows.

85 sts.
Cont straight from chart until all 100 rows have been completed. Bind off with M.

FRONT
Work as back until 85 rows of chart have been completed.

Neck Shaping
Cont from chart thus:

Next row (right side) Pat 31 sts, turn.
Cont on these sts only for 1st side and leave rem sts on a spare needle.
Dec 1 st at neck edge on the next 5 rows. 26 sts.
Cont straight from chart until all 100 rows have been completed. Bind off with M.
Next row With right side facing, sl center 23 sts on to a stitch holder, rejoin yarn to inner end of rem 31 sts

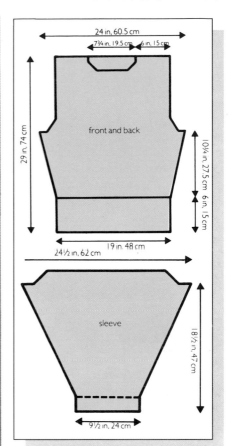

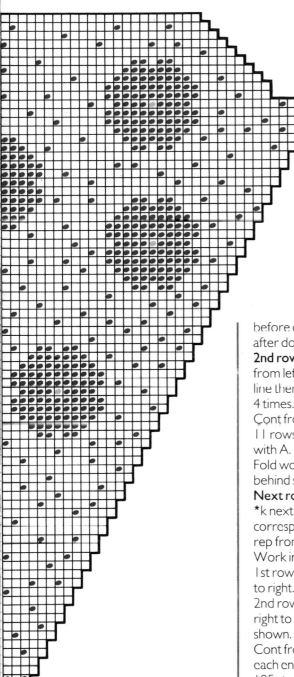

and pat to end.
Complete to match 1st side.

SLEEVES
With No. 7 needles and A, cast on
41 sts for cuff.
St-st 12 rows.
Change to No. 8 needles. P 2 rows.
Cont in st-st from Chart 3 thus:
1st row (right side) Reading 1st row of
chart from right to left, k the 10 sts

before dotted line 4 times, then k st
after dotted line.
2nd row Reading 2nd row of chart
from left to right, p st before dotted
line then p the 10 sts after dotted line
4 times.
Cont from chart in this way until all
11 rows have been worked. P 1 row
with A.
Fold work in half with cast-on edge
behind sts on needle.
Next row (close hem) With A,
*k next st from needle tog with
corresponding st from cast on edge;
rep from * to end.
Work in st-st from Chart 4 thus:
1st row is a p row, read chart from left
to right.
2nd row is a k row, read chart from
right to left, inc at each end of row as
shown.
Cont from chart in this way, inc 1 st at
each end of every k row until there are
105 sts. Pat 3 rows straight, thus
completing 67 rows of chart.

Cap Shaping
Bind off 4 sts at beg of next 2 rows.
Dec 1 st at each end of next 8 rows.
81 sts.
Bind off loosely with M.

NECKBAND
Mark center 33 sts on bind-off edge of
back for neck.
Join right shoulder seam.
With No. 8 needles and A, pick up
and k 18 sts evenly down left front
neck, k across 23 sts at center front,

pick up and k 18 sts up right front neck
and 32 sts across back neck. 91 sts.
P 1 row.
Cont in st-st from Chart 3 thus:
1st row (right side) Reading 1st row of
chart from right to left, k the 10 sts
before dotted line 9 times, then k st
after dotted line.
2nd row Reading 2nd row of chart
from left to right, p st before dotted
line then p the 10 sts after dotted line
9 times.
Cont from chart in this way until all
11 rows have been worked.
P 2 rows with A.
Change to No. 7 needles.
Beg with a p row, st-st 10 rows with A.
Fold neckband in half on to wrong side
and * loosely sew 1 st from needle to
corresponding st of pick up row; rep
from * to end.

FINISHING
Press lightly. Join left shoulder and
neckband seam – join outer and inner
edges of neckband separately. With
center of bind-off edge of sleeves to
shoulder seams, set in sleeves. Join side
seams carefully matching pat on hip
bands. Join sleeve seams joining outer
and inner edges of cuffs separately.

TURKESTAN

TASHKENT

STYLISED EASTERN FLOWERS SPREAD OVER A BIG MOHAIR JACKET AND DRAW ATTENTION TO SHOULDERS. DESIGNED BY LESLEY STANFIELD

MATERIALS

Argyll Finesse Mohair
18 × 25 g balls Mandrake (M)
3 × 25 g balls Sirocco (A)
3 × 25 g balls Raspberry (B)
3 × 25 g balls Aubretia (C)
1 × 25 g ball Antique Gold (D)
Pair each No. 8 and No. 10 knitting needles
Pair large detachable shoulder pads

MEASUREMENTS

One size, to fit up to bust 42 in, 107 cm
Actual measurement – 52½ in, 134 cm approx
Length – 30¼ in, 77 cm approx
Sleeve length – 12½ in, 32 cm approx

GAUGE

13 sts and 17 rows to 4 in (10 cm) over st-st on No. 10 needles

ABBREVIATIONS

alt – alternate; beg – beginning; cm – centimeters; cont – continue; dec –decrease; foll – following; in – inches; inc – increase; k – knit; p – purl; pat – pattern; psso – pass slipped stitch over; rem – remain(ing); rep – repeat; sl – slip; st(s) – stitch(es); st-st – stockinette stitch; tbl – through back of loops

BACK

With No. 8 needles and M, cast on 89 sts.
Beg k, work 7 rows in st-st.
K 1 row to mark hemline.
Change to No. 10 needles.
Cont in st-st from Chart 1, carrying color(s) not in use loosely across wrong side on multi-colour rows, thus:
1st row (right side) Reading row 1 of chart from right to left, k 8 pat sts 11 times, then k last st.

2nd row Reading row 2 of chart from left to right, p first st, then p 8 pat sts 11 times.
3rd to 8th rows As 1st and 2nd rows but working rows 3 to 8 of chart *.
Cont in st-st from Chart 2, reading rows alternately from right to left, then left to right. Only carry color not in use across small areas (e.g. some stems). Otherwise work with separate lengths of yarns, twisting them at each color change (see color knitting notes on page 108. Small areas of color may be duplicate stitched afterwards, if preferred.
Cont until row 56 has been completed.

Raglan Shaping

Cont from chart, dec 1 st at each end of row 57 and every foll alt row until row 98 has been completed (work k 2 tog at beg and k 2 tog tbl at end for each dec). 47 sts.
Cont from chart, dec 1 st at each end of every row until row 110 has been completed. Leave rem 23 sts on a stitch holder.

LEFT FRONT

With No. 8 needles and M, cast on 41 sts.
Work as back to * but work the pat sts 5 times **.
Work rows 1 to 56 of Chart 3.

TURKESTAN

CHART I

begin here ▲

CHART 2

110

56

KEY TO ALL CHARTS

□ M

▣ A

▣ B

▣ C

▣ D

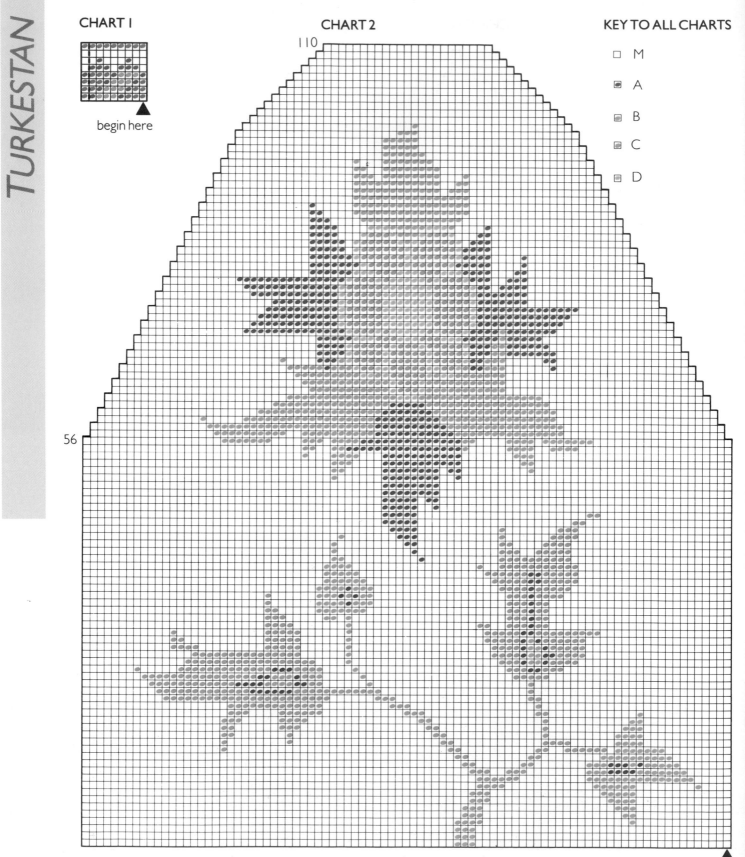

begin here ▲

CHART 4   CHART 3

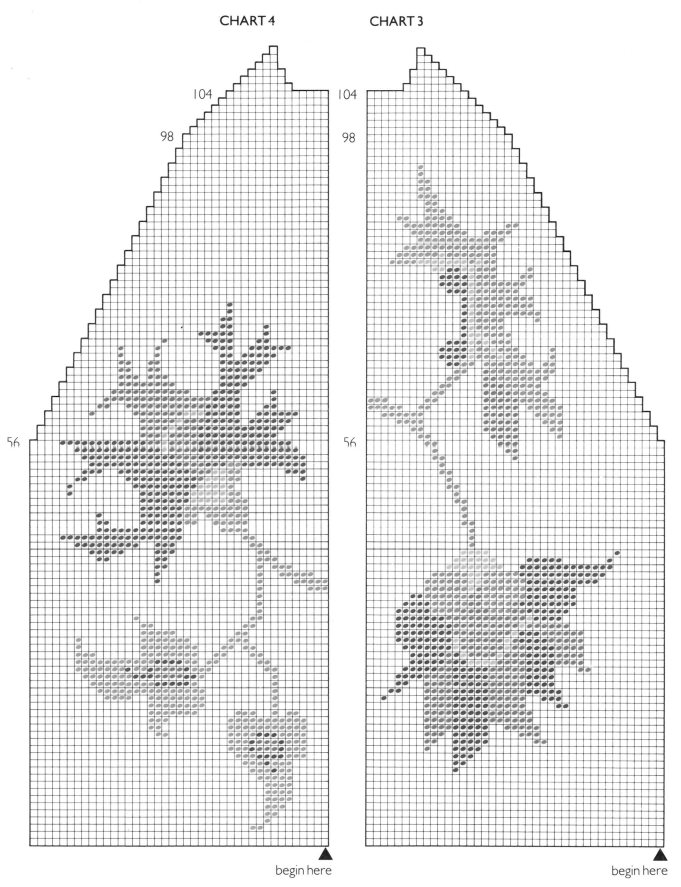

104   104

98   98

56   56

begin here   begin here

Raglan Shaping

Cont from chart, dec I st at beg of row 57 and every foll alt row until row 98 has been completed. 20 sts.
Dec I st at raglan edge on every row until row 104 has been completed. 14 sts.
105th row K 2 tog, k 7, sl rem 5 sts on to a safety pin.
***Dec I st at neck edge on next row and on the foll alt row, AND AT THE

SAME TIME, dec I st at raglan edge on every row until 2 sts rem.
P 2 tog and fasten off.

RIGHT FRONT

Work as left front to ******.
Work rows I to 56 of Chart 4.

Raglan Shaping

Cont from chart, dec I st at end of row

57 and every foll alt row until row 98 has been completed. 20 sts.
Dec I st at raglan edge on every row until row 104 has been completed.
14 sts.
105th row Break yarn, sl 5 sts on to a safety pin, rejoin yarn and k 7, k 2 tog tbl.
Complete to match left front from *******.

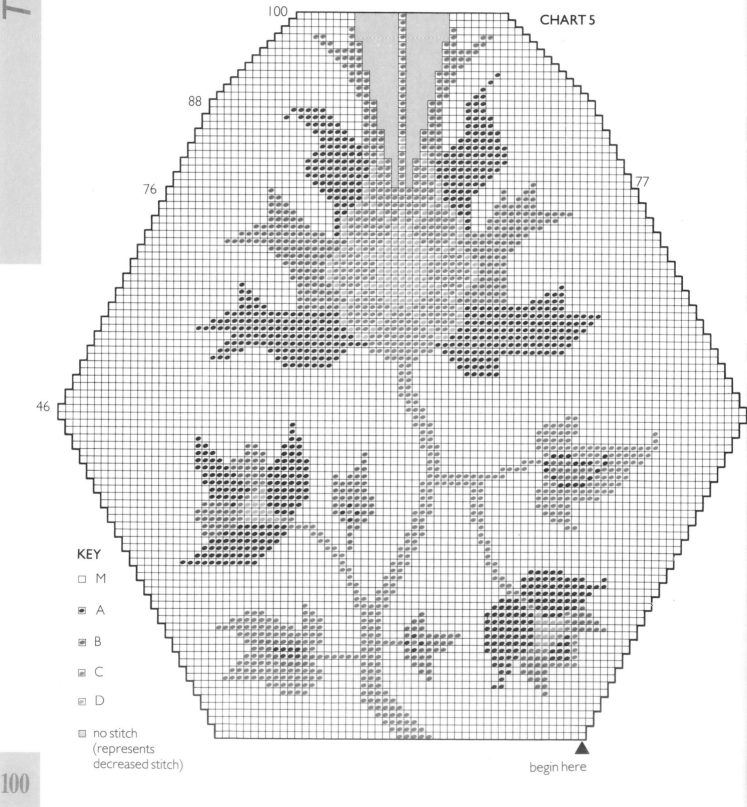

CHART 5

KEY

☐ M

▨ A

▨ B

▨ C

▨ D

☐ no stitch (represents decreased stitch)

begin here

SLEEVES

With No. 8 needles and M, cast on 49 sts. Work as back to * but work the 8 pat sts 6 times.
Cont in st-st from Chart 5, inc 1 st at each end of row 1 and every foll alt row (row 1 of 51 sts includes increases). Cont from chart until row 46 has been completed. 95 sts.

Raglan Shaping

Cont from chart, dec 1 st at each end of row 47 and every foll alt row until row 76 has been completed. 65 sts.
77th row K 2 tog M, k 12 M, 1 C, 6 M, 6 B, 1 D, 2 A, sl 1, k 1 A, psso, k 1 A, k 2 tog A, 2 A, 1 D, 7 B, 18 M, k 2 tog tbl M. Ignoring shaded areas which represent decreased sts, cont from chart, working 1 dec either side of center st on every 4th row, AND AT THE SAME TIME, dec at each end of every right-side row until row 88 has been completed. 47 sts.
Cont to dec at center as before, AND AT THE SAME TIME, dec at each end of every row until row 100 has been completed.
Leave rem 17 sts on a stitch holder.

NECKBAND

Join raglan seams.
With right side facing, using No. 10 needles and M, k 5 sts from right front safety pin, pick up and k 5 sts up right front neck, k 17 sts of right sleeve, 23 sts of back neck and 17 sts of left sleeve, pick up and k 5 sts down left front neck then k across 5 sts on left front safety pin. 77 sts.
Dec row P 10, *p 2 tog, p 3; rep from * 10 times, p 2 tog, p 10. 65 sts.
Work the 8 rows of Chart 1 as for back, working the 8 pat sts 8 times.
Change to No. 8 needles and M. K 1 row. K 1 row to mark hemline.
Beg K, st-st 9 rows. Bind off.

LEFT FRONT BAND

With right side facing, using No. 10 needles and M, pick up and k 97 sts evenly between neckband hemline and lower hemline.
Beg p, and working from left to right on row 1, work 8 rows of Chart 1 as for back, working the 8 pat sts 12 times.
Change to No. 8 needles and M.
P 1 row. P 1 row to mark hemline.
Beg p, st-st 8 rows. Bind off loosely.
To neaten upper and lower edges –
with right side facing, using No. 10 needles and M, pick up and k 7 sts along pat section only. Bind off knitwise.
Work right front band to match.

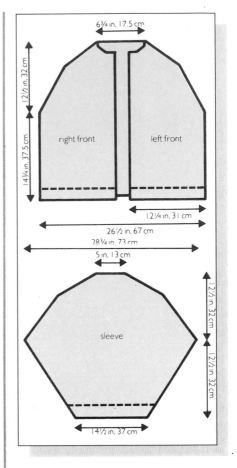

SHOULDER PAD COVERS

Make 2 With No. 8 needles and M, cast on 69 sts.
Decreasing 1 st at each end of 3rd row and on the foll alt row, work 4 rows in k 1, p 1 rib, then st-st 2 rows. 65 sts.
7th row K 2 tog, k 28, sl 1, k 1, psso, k 1, k 2 tog, k 28, k 2 tog tbl.
8th row P.
The last 2 rows correspond to rows 77 and 78 of Chart 5.
Cont to shape as chart until 17 sts rem, but omitting color changes. Bind off.

FINISHING

Press carefully. Turn down neckband hem and sew down. Join side and sleeve seams. Turn up lower hem and sew down. Turn in hems of front bands and sew down along bind-off edge, then whipstitch at neck and lower edges. Turn in sleeve hems and sew down. On wrong side place shoulder pad covers at top of sleeves with p sides tog and sew along raglan seams and at neckband edge. Leave rib edge open to insert detachable shoulder pads.

TASHKENT

E·C·L·I·P·S·E

WHITE HOT

ECLIPSE

UNDERSTATED SIMPLICITY IN FRONT CHANGES DRAMATICALLY AT THE BACK, WHERE CONTINUOUS RIB EDGINGS ARE LINKED TO HOLD THE TWO SIDES TOGETHER – AN ELEGANT WAY TO MAKE AN EXIT. DESIGNED BY PHYLLIS SANBAR

MATERIALS
5 (5, 6) × 50 g balls Sirdar Sombrero
Pair No. 3 knitting needles
2 spare needles
2 stitch holders

MEASUREMENTS
To fit bust 34 (36, 38) in, 86 (91, 97) cm
Actual measurement – 38½ (42, 45) in, 98 (107, 115) cm
Length – 23 in, 58 cm
Figures in parenthesis are for larger sizes

GAUGE
24 sts and 32 rows to 4 in (10 cm) over st-st on No. 3 needles

ABBREVIATIONS
alt – alternate; beg – beginning; cm – centimeters; cont – continue; dec – decrease; foll – following; in – inches; inc – increase; k – knit; p – purl; rem – remaining; rep – repeat; sl – slip; st(s) – stitch(es); st-st – stockinette stitch

FRONT
With No. 3 needles, cast on 90 (98, 106) sts.

1st rib row (right side) K 2, *p 2, k 2; rep from * to end.

2nd rib row P 2, *k 2, p 2; rep from * to end.

Rep last 2 rows 6 times, then work 1st rib row again.

Inc row Rib 0 (2, 3), * inc in next st, rib 2; rep from * to last 0 (0, 1) st, rib 0 (0, 1); 120 (130, 140) sts.

Beg with a k row, work 90 rows in st-st.

Armband Shaping

1st row Cast on 4 sts, work k 2, p 2 across cast-on sts, k to end.

2nd row Cast on 4 sts, work p 2, k 2 across cast-on sts, p to last 4 sts, p 2, k 2.

3rd row Cast on 4 sts, work k 2, p 2 across cast-on sts, work as set to end.

4th row Cast on 4 sts, work p 2, k 2 across cast-on sts, work as set to end.

Rep 3rd and 4th rows 3 times, thus a total of 20 sts have been cast on at each end and these are worked in rib. 160 (170, 180) sts.

Keeping 20 sts at each end in rib and rem sts in st-st, work 59 rows.

Neck Shaping

1st row (wrong side) Work 67 (72, 77) sts, bind off next 26 sts, work to end.

Cont on last 67 (72, 77) sts only for 1st side and leave rem sts on a spare needle.

Dec 1 st at neck edge on the next 5 rows, then on the foll 2 alt rows. Work 1 row straight.

Bind off rem 60 (65, 70) sts.

With right side facing, rejoin yarn to inner end of sts on spare needle and complete to match 1st side.

BACK

With No. 3 needles, cast on 50 (54, 58) sts for left back.

Work 1st and 2nd rib rows of front 7 times, then work 1st rib row again.

Inc row *Rib 1, inc in next st, rib 1; rep from * 9 (10, 11) times, rib 20 (21, 22). 60 (65, 70) sts.

Cont in st-st with ribbed border thus:

1st row (right side) Rib 20, k to end.

2nd row P to last 20 sts, rib to end.

Rep 1st and 2nd rows 24 times.

*Next row Rib 18 turn and leave rem 42 (47, 52) sts on a spare needle.

Rib 8 rows on these 18 sts then sl the 18 sts on to a stitch holder. Do not break off yarn*.

With No. 3 needles, cast on 50 (54, 58) sts for right back.

Work 1st and 2nd rib rows of front 7 times, then work 1st rib row again.

Inc row Rib 20 (21, 22), *rib 1, inc in next st, rib 1; rep from * to end. 60 (65, 70) sts.

Cont in st-st with ribbed border thus:

1st row (right side) K to last 20 sts, rib to end.

2nd row Rib 20 sts, P to end.

Rep 1st and 2nd rows 24 times, then work 1st row again.

Next row Rib 18 turn and leave rem 42 (47, 52) sts on a spare needle.

Rib 8 rows on these 18 sts.

Joining row Rib across these 18 sts, then work p 2, k 40 (45, 50) across sts on the left back spare needle. 60 (65, 70) sts**.

Work 9 rows as set, then rep from * to *.

Joining row With wrong side facing, rib across 18 sts on 1st stitch holder, then working behind 2nd stitch holder work k 2 and p 40 (45, 50) across sts on right back spare needle.

Work 9 rows as set, then rep from ** to ** noting that on joining row, after working rib, work behind sts on stitch holder.

Work 9 rows as set, then rep from * to *.

Joining row With wrong side facing and working behind spare needles and last stitch holder, rib across 18 sts on 1st stitch holder then k 2 and p 40 (45, 50) across sts on right back spare needle.

Work 9 rows as set, then rep from ** to ** noting that on joining row work behind sts on stitch holder.

Work 20 rows as set, thus ending at side edge.

Armband Shaping

1st row Cast on 4 sts, work p 2, k 2 across cast-on sts, p to last 20 sts, rib 20.

2nd row Rib 20, k to last 4 sts, p 2, k 2.

3rd row Cast on 4 sts, work p 2, k 2 across cast-on sts, p 2, k 2, p to last 20 sts, rib 20.

4th row Rib 20, k to last 8 sts, p 2, k 2, p 2, k 2.

Cont in this way, casting on 4 sts at beg of every wrong-side row until a total of 20 sts have been cast on and worked in rib. 80 (85, 90) sts.

Work 71 rows as set, thus ending at armband edge.

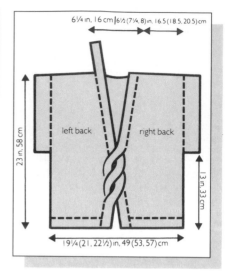

Shoulder Shaping

Bind off 60 (65, 70) sts, rib to end.

Rib 50 rows on rem 20 sts.

Bind off in rib.

With wrong side facing and working behind left back, return to 18 sts on stitch holder, rib 18, then work k 2, p 40 (45, 50) across sts of right back.

Work 18 rows as set, thus ending at side edge.

Armband Shaping

1st row Cast on 4 sts, work k 2, p 2 across cast-on sts, k to last 20 sts, rib 20.

2nd row Rib 20, p to last 4 sts, k 2, p 2.

3rd row Cast on 4 sts, work k 2, p 2 across cast-on sts, k 2, p 2, k to last 20 sts, rib 20.

4t row Rib 20, p to last 8 sts, k 2, p 2, k 2, p 2.

Cont in this way, casting on 4 sts at beg of every right-side row until a total of 20 sts have been cast on and worked in rib. 80 (85, 90) sts.

Work 71 rows as set, thus ending at armband edge.

Shoulder Shaping

Bind off all 80 (85, 90) sts.

FINISHING

Join left shoulder seam. Join right shoulder seam extending seam across bind-off sts of ribbed borders. Sew free row-ends of ribbed border around front neck. Join side and armband seams. Press seams lightly.

MERIDIAN

A SOFT RIBBED TUBE WITH A SINGLE INTERTWINING CABLE AND A CLOSE-FITTING TURTLE-NECK IS AN ESSENTIAL PART OF A SUMMER WARDROBE. DESIGNED BY CAROLINE INGRAM

MATERIALS

8 (8, 9) × 50 g balls Jarol Cotton 2000 Double Knitting
Pair each No. 1, No. 2 and No. 4 knitting needles
Cable needle

MEASUREMENTS

To fit bust 32 (34, 36) in, 81 (86, 91) cm
Actual measurement – 31 (34, 36) in, 78 (86, 91) cm, slightly stretched
Length – 24 in, 60 cm
Figures in parenthesis are for larger sizes

GAUGE

26 sts and 30 rows to 4 in (10 cm) measured over slightly stretched rib on No. 4 needles

ABBREVIATIONS

beg – beginning; c 6 b – sl next 3 sts on to cable needle and hold at back, k 3 then k 3 from cable needle; c 6 f – sl next 3 sts on to cable needle and hold at front, k 3 then k 3 from cable needle; c 12 b – sl next 6 sts on to cable needle and hold at back, k 6 then k 6 from cable needle; c 12 f – sl next 6 sts on to cable needle and hold at front, k 6 then k 6 from cable needle; cm – centimeters; cont – continue; dec – decrease; in – inches; inc – increase; k – knit; m 1 – make 1 st by picking up the strand between sts and k it through the back of the loop; p – purl; pat – pattern; rem – remain(ing); rep – repeat; sl – slip; st(s) – stitch(es); tog – together.
Work instructions in square brackets the number of times given

BACK

With No. 1 needles, cast on 102 (110, 118) sts.
1st rib row (right side) P 2, *k 2, p 2; rep from * to end.
2nd rib row K 2, *p 2, k 2; rep from * to end.
Rep 1st and 2nd rib rows for 2 in (5 cm), ending with a 1st rib row.
Inc row Rib 49 (53, 57), m 1, rib 4, m 1, rib 49 (53, 57). 104 (112, 120) sts.
Change to No. 4 needles.
Cont in pat thus:
1st row (right side) K 4 (0, 4), [p 2, k 6] 5 (6, 6) times, p 2, k 6, p 1, k 5, p 2 [k 6, p 2] 5 (6, 6) times, k 4 (0, 4).

2nd row P 4 (0, 4), [k 2, p 6] 5 (6, 6) times, k 2, p 5, k 1, p 6, k 2 [p 6, k 2] 5 (6, 6) times, p 4 (0, 4).
3rd row K 4 (0, 4), [p 2, k 6] 5 (6, 6) times, p 2, c 6 f, p 1, k 5, p 2, [k 6, p 2] 5 (6, 6) times, k 4 (0, 4).
4th row As 2nd row.
5th to 8th rows As 1st to 4th rows.
9th and 10th rows As 1st and 2nd rows.
11th row K 4 (0, 4), [p 2, k 6] 5 (6, 6) times, p 2, c 12 b, p 2, [k 6, p 2] 5 (6, 6) times, k 4 (0, 4).
12th row P 4 (0, 4), [k 2, p 6] 5 (6, 6) times, k 2, p 6, k 1, p 5, k 2, [p 6, k 2] 5 (6, 6) times, p 4 (0, 4).

13th row K 4 (0, 4), [p 2, k 6] 5 (6, 6) times, p 2, k 5, p 1, k 6, p 2, [k 6, p 2] 5 (6, 6) times, k 4 (0, 4).
14th row As 12th row.
15th row K 4 (0, 4), [p 2, k 6] 5 (6, 6) times, p 2, k 5, p 1, c 6 b, p 2, [k 6, p 2] 5 (6, 6) times, k 4 (0, 4).
16th row As 12th row.
17th to 28th rows Rep 13th to 16th rows 3 times.
29th and 30th rows As 13th and 14th rows.
31st row K 4 (0, 4), [p 2, k 6] 5 (6, 6) times, p 2, c 12 f, p 2, [k 6, p 2] 5 (6, 6) times, k 4 (0, 4).
32nd row As 2nd row.
33rd to 40th row Rep 1st to 4th rows twice.
These 40 rows form pat.
Pat straight until back measures 14¼ in (36 cm), ending with a wrong-side row.

Armhole Shaping

Keeping pat correct, bind off 5 (6, 7) sts at beg of next 2 rows.
Dec 1 st at each end of every row until 74 (76, 78) sts rem.**
Pat straight until work measures 22½ in, (57 cm), ending with a wrong-side row.

Neck Shaping

1st row Pat 25 (26, 27) sts, turn.
Cont on these sts only, leaving rem sts on spare needle.
Dec 1 st at neck edge on next 10 rows. 15 (16, 17) sts.
Bind off loosely.
Next row With right side facing, sl center 24 sts on to a stitch holder, rejoin yarn to inner edge of rem 25 (26, 27) sts and pat to end. Complete

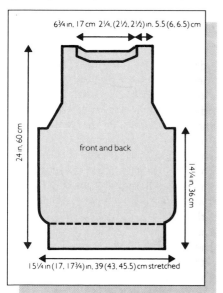

6¾ in, 17 cm 2¼, (2½, 2½) in, 5.5 (6, 6.5) cm

24 in, 60 cm

front and back

14¼ in, 36 cm

15¼ in (17, 17¾) in, 39 (43, 45.5) cm stretched

to match 1st side.

FRONT

Work as back to **.
Pat straight until front measures 21 in (53 cm), ending with a wrong-side row.

Neck Shaping

1st row Pat 29 (30, 31) sts, turn.
Cont on these sts only, leaving rem sts on a spare needle.
Dec 1 st at neck edge on next 14 rows. 15 (16, 17) sts.
Pat straight until front matches back to shoulder.
Bind off loosely.
Next row With right side facing, sl center 16 sts on to a stitch holder, rejoin yarn to inner edge of rem 29 (30, 31) sts and pat to end.
Complete to match 1st side.

COLLAR

Join right shoulder seam.
With right side facing, using No. 1 needles, pick up and k 28 sts evenly down left front neck, pat across 16 sts at center front thus: p 2, k 2, p 2, k 1, k 2 tog, p 2, k 2 tog, k 1, p 2; pick up and k 28 sts up right front neck, pick up and k 14 sts down right back neck, pat across 24 sts at center back thus: [p 2, k 2] twice, p 2, k 1, k 2 tog, p 2, k 2 tog, k 1, p 2, k 2, p 2; pick up and k 14 sts up left back neck. 120 sts.
Work 4 in (10 cm) in p 2, k 2 rib.
Change to No. 2 needles.
Cont straight until rib measures 7½ in (19 cm).
Bind off loosely in rib.

ARMBANDS

Join left shoulder and collar seam, reversing collar seam for last 5½ in (14 cm) to allow for turn-over.
With right side facing and using No. 2 needles, pick up and k 150 (154, 158) sts evenly around armhole.
Work 5 rows k 2, p 2 rib as given for back.
Bind off in rib.

FINISHING

Join side and armband seams. Press seams only.

BACK TO BASICS

SIZING

As you can't try on a design before you start to knit and you don't have a paper pattern for guidance, do look critically at the measurement and proportions of what you intend to make. The fit of these designs varies so much – from a singlet that is under-sized and intended to cling to several deliberately over-sized sweaters – that actual measurements of the finished garments have been given throughout. Look at all the figures given and, if you're in doubt, make a comparison by measuring clothes you already have.

GAUGE

Of course, if your garment is to be the size specified it must be knitted to the correct gauge. The idea of knitting a sample square before starting on the whole seems awfully tedious but it is essential for accuracy. It is equally important to measure the finished square scrupulously. Too many knitters (and designers) measure the gauge that they want to see. The best way is to count the rows and stitches stated in the gauge guide and mark these with pins. Then measure between the markers and see if you have the correct length. If you are over the given measurement use a smaller needle size, if you are under use a larger needle size. Remember that the stated needle size is only a recommendation.

SHOULDER PADS

Many of these designs are intended to take shoulder pads, so the width of shoulder and depth of armhole have been calculated accordingly. Where the shoulder is a neat, squared-off shape a conventional pair of pads is appropriate. But some of the really large shoulders, especially the raglans, are designed to take the new moulded shapes with adhesive strip which are sold in most department stores and specialist shops. It's very convenient to

detach them for storage. Big shoulders also have the advantage of making the waist and hips look smaller by comparison.

CHARTS

These are used to give the pattern in most types of color knitting. Occasionally they are also used to convey stitch patterns. If you haven't used them before don't be put off. Once you have mastered the key you will find you have a very clear visual explanation of the stitch.

COLOR KNITTING

In Fair Isle technique with color patterns repeating along a row, the color not in use is carried across the back of the work. Always carry the colors in the same sequence and don't pull the strand too tight. Spreading out the last few stitches on the right hand needle before carrying will help. If the yarn not in use has to be carried over groups of more than six or seven stitches it's usually advisable to catch it in at intervals. To catch it in, take the second color over the color in use just before making a stitch. Take care to make a firm stitch and again, don't take the yarn across too tightly.

With large areas of color it's better to use the motif or intarsia technique. That is, use a separate small ball of yarn for each area of color. If there are many areas being worked simultaneously it's a good idea to wind a few meters of yarn on to small plastic or cardboard bobbins. Weaving in the ends afterwards is preferable to untangling a lot of yarn as you work. At every color change the two yarns should be twisted to prevent a hole forming. This simply means crossing one yarn over the other between stitches to lock the two areas together.

Duplicate stitch is embroidery over the top of a stitch to change the color. If the knitted stitch is seen as a V, the needle is taken through the point of

the V from the back, then under the two strands of the stitch above from right to left, then back into the point of the V from front to back. This stitch should duplicate the knitted stitch exactly.

FINISHING

The iron symbol on the ball band indicates if the yarn can be pressed and at what temperature. Do read the ball band carefully. As a general rule, natural fibers can be damp-pressed but synthetic fibers are better dry-pressed or not pressed at all. To damp-press your work, pin out the pieces, right side down. Using the measurement diagrams as a guide, square the pieces up so that rows and stitches run at perfect right angles. Press, using a thin, damp cloth under a warm iron. It's impossible to revive over-pressed work but under-pressing is not making the most of your knitting. Don't press ribs at all and be careful not to flatten textured stitches. Press seams as you sew them up.

AFTERCARE

Keep a ball band and refer to it for washing and dry cleaning instructions. It's better not to use harsh detergents even if a yarn is machine washable. A cool or cold water wash is suitable for most hand knitting. Don't wring out, just squeeze gently and dry flat or spin dry in a pillow case. Never hang knitting up, especially when it's made heavier by being wet. When the garment is damp it should be eased into shape.

Knitting is a very elastic fabric and its shape and texture can be drastically altered by washing and pressing. Do make sure that you improve yours!

LIST OF SUPPLIERS

In case of difficulty obtaining any of the products mentioned please contact the company concerned. If you write, please enclose a stamped addressed envelope. Mail order details can usually be supplied in addition to information about stockists.

ANNY BLATT
Anny Blatt
24770 Crestview Court
Farmington Hills, MI 48018

ARGYLL
Estelle Designs & Sales, Ltd.
1135 Queen Street East
Toronto, Ontario
Canada M4M 1K9

AVOCET
Estelle Designs & Sales, Ltd.
1135 Queen Street East
Toronto, Ontario
Canada CD M4M 1K9

EMU
Plymouth Yarn Co. Inc.
P.O. Box 28
500 Lafayette St.
Bristol, PA 19007

GEORGES PICAUD
Merino Wool Co. Inc.
230 Fifth Avenue
New York, NY 10001

JAEGER
Susan Bates, Inc.
212 Middlesex Avenue
Chester, CT 06412

LISTER
J.H. Imports Ltd.
P.O. Box 326
Millersville, MD 21108

PATONS
Susan Bates, Inc.
212 Middlesex Avenue
Chester, CT 06412

PHILDAR
Phildar, Inc.
6438 Dawson Blvd.
Norcross, GA 30093

PINGOUIN
Pingouin
P.O. Box 100
Jamestown, SC 29453

ROBIN
Plymouth Yarn Co. Inc.
P.O. Box 28
500 Lafayette St.
Bristol, PA 19007

ROWAN
Westminster Trading
5 Northern Blvd.
Amherst, NH 03031

SCHACHENMAYR
c/o Leisure Arts
P.O. Box 5595
Little Rock, ARK 72215

SCHEEPJESWOL
Scheepjeswol USA
1299 Trade Zone Dr.
Ronkonama, NY 11779

SIRDAR
c/o Kendex Corp.
P.O. Box 4347
Westlake Village, CA 91359

3 SUISSES
Bucilla
Sales Service Dept.
150 Meadowlands Pkway.
Secaucus, NJ 07094

SUNBEAM
c/o Phillips
P.O. Box 146
Port St. Joe, FL 32456

TWILLEYS
2120 Broadway
Lubbock, TX 79401

ACKNOWLEDGMENTS

A guide to the clothes and accessories featured:

ROSE QUARTZ (page 8)
suit and earrings: Fenwick, New Bond Street, London W1; belt: Hobbs, South Molton Street, London W1; bracelet: Detail, Endell Street, London WC2

AMETHYST (page 11)
suit: Whistles, St Christopher's Place, London W1; jewellery: Michaela Frey, South Molton Street, London W1; gloves: Dents from Attitudes at Moss Bros

BON CHIC (page 14)
necklaces and bracelets: John Lewis, London W1; earrings: Pink Soda at Miss Selfridge; skirt and polo neck jumper: Fenwick; velvet gloves: Dents; shoes: Hobbs; beret: The Hat Shop, Neal Street, London WC2

SYCAMORE (page 18)
breeches: Laurence Corner, Hampstead Road, London NW1; hat: Blax, Sicilian Avenue, London WC2; lace blouse: Capricorn, Kensington Park Road, London W11; brooch: John Wind at Harvey Nichols; stick: Fulton; gloves: Dents

SILVER BIRCH (page 22)
breeches: Laurence Corner; earrings: Blax; stick: Fulton; string-back gloves: Dents; hat: model's own

NORTHERN LIGHTS (page 26)
leggings: Fitness Centre, Langley Street, London WC2; gloves: Fenwick

FINE ROMANCE (page 30)
earrings: Detail; bracelet: Blax; fabrics: John Lewis

KNIGHTSBRIDGE (page 34)
beret, polo neck jumper and tights: Fenwick; brooch: Detail; gloves: Dents; shoes: Hobbs

KENSINGTON (page 38)
beret and tights: Fenwick; earrings: Detail

BELGRAVIA (page 41)
scarf and tights: Fenwick; bracelets: Detail

SUPERSAMPLER (page 43)
leggings: Hilary Bockham at Zone, Harvey Nichols; sunglasses and gloves: Fenwick; shoes: Robot; mittens: model's own

CRIMSON (page 48)
silk skirt: Linda Powell, 62 Triton Road, London SE21; bracelet: Michaela Frey; earrings: Van Peterson, Walton Street, London SW3

SCARLET (page 51)
dress: Benetton; jet bracelets: Michaela Frey; earrings: Van Peterson

VERMILION (page 55)
dress: Whistles; earrings: Van Peterson

PERFECT PARTNERS (page 58)
skirt: Whistles; jewellery: Michaela Frey; brocade hat: The Hat Shop

DELHI (page 62)
skirt: Jeffrey Rogers; bracelets: John Lewis; hat: The Hat Shop

MADRAS (page 66)
lace skirt: Linda Powell; jewellery: Van Peterson

JAIPUR (page 69)
leggings: Jeffrey Rogers; hat: Warehouse

FIFTIES FOREVER (page 71)
watch: Detail; bracelets: Extras at Hyper Hyper; belt: Fenwick; vest and jeans: model's own

MARLBOROUGH (page 74)
trousers, shirt, tie and braces: Blax; brooch worn as tie pin: Fenwick

WINCHESTER (page 78)
trousers: Fenwick; socks: Blax; mittens: Laurence Corner; shoes: Hobbs; hat, scarf, raincoat: model's own

ETON (page 81)
shorts: Laurence corner; polo neck sweater: Paul Smith, Floral Street, London WC2; watch: Fenwick; tights: Aristoc; spectacles: model's own

HARROW (page 84)
belt: Mulberry, Gees Court, London W1; scarf: The Scotch House, Knightsbridge, London SW3; trousers, earrings: model's own

DENIM DAYS (page 87)
jeans: Falmers; shirt: C17, James Street, London W1; beret: Laura Ashley; gloves: Laurence Corner; bag and scarf: models own

BOKHARA (page 90)
shirt: Benetton; shawl: The Scotch House; jewellery: Catalyst at Hyper Hyper; bowler hat: The Hat Shop; tights: Mary quant; boots: Robot

TASHKENT (page 96)
skirt: Benetton; underskirt: Fenwick; blouse: Consumer Guide at Jones, Kings Road, London SW3; shawl: Capricorn; jewellery: Catalyst; gloves: Dents; boots: Robot; tights: Mary Quant; hat: The Hat Shop

ECLIPSE (page 102)
skirt: Benetton; earrings: Detail; bracelet: John Lewis

MERIDIAN (page 105)
skirt: Benetton; bracelets and earrings: Detail; hat: The Hat Shop

A·C·K·N·O·W·L·E·D·G·M·E·N·T·S

The book was designed by Polly Dawes

Photography by
Tony Boase: 18, 21, 22, 23, 43, 46, 47, 74, 75, 76, 78, 80, 81, 82, 84, 87, 88
Jill Green and Neil Phillips of Pinsharp: front cover, 8, 10, 11, 13, 30, 31, 58, 59, 61, 90, 91, 96, 97, 101
Heinz Lautenbacher: 48, 49, 50, 51, 54, 55, 56, 62, 63, 64, 66, 67, 68, 69, 102, 103, 105, 106
Francesca Sullivan: 14, 15, 16, 26, 27, 29, 34, 35, 36, 38, 39, 41, 42, 71, 72

Photographic styling by Marie Willey
Make-up by Kim Jacob of Pin-Up
Hair styled by Jaffa of Pin-Up

Instructions written and styled by Sue Horan
Instructions checked by Marilyn Wilson
Charts and diagrams by Jeremy Firth

ACKNOWLEDGMENTS

112